Working in the City

Working in the City

Mike Poole

Working in the City: A guide to starting a successful career in the City

This edition published in 2013 by Trotman Publishing, a division of Crimson Publishing Ltd, Westminster House, Kew Road, Richmond, Surrey TW9 2ND.

© Trotman Publishing 2013

Author: Mike Poole

The rights of Mike Poole to be identified as the author of this work have been asserted by him in accordance with the Copyright, Designs and Patents Act, 1988.

British Library Cataloguing in Publication Data
A catalogue record for this book is available from the British Library.

ISBN 978 1 84455 516 1

Typeset by IDSUK (DataConnection) Ltd
Printed and bound in the UK by Ashford Colour Press, Gosport, Hants

Contents

Contents

Contents

Introduction

This book is for anyone thinking about trying to become 'something in the City'. It will explain the main types of different jobs the different finance-related sectors that are available in the City, and how to go about starting your career in:

- retail banking
- investment banking
- insurance
- accounting
- management consultancy
- other jobs in the City.

It will offer an insight into the different sectors, some of the main companies involved and what the roles involve, as well as offering advice on how to get your first graduate job and develop your career. It will also try to give a flavour of the sort of lifestyle that goes with these jobs because, while they can be very rewarding, they are not for everyone.

Some people make their career in the City; many more use the City as a valuable training ground for working successfully in other spheres. It is not unusual, for example, for an executive in banking to go into industry, or for someone in management consultancy to go into a senior role in the sector in which they were consulting (manufacturing or government, for example). The discipline and skills learned in the City – and the contacts made there – can be extremely valuable in a wide variety of settings.

One of the first things to determine is what you want to do. The current market preference is for specialists, not generalists. Each of the sectors outlined above has subsets within it and almost all of them require different skills, qualifications, networks and experience. Trying to go for several at once may mean that you don't quite achieve what you need for any of them. The earlier you decide which sector you want to undertake, and why, the stronger your chances of success. Above all,

Introduction

whichever you choose, you are going to be spending the majority of your time on it for at least the next few years – so if it is something that you enjoy, that's probably going to help a lot.

Hopefully, this book will help you decide.

1

What is 'the City'?

'The City' means different things to different people. Since we're devoting a book to careers in the City, it would be good to start by agreeing what we mean.

Originally, of course, 'the City' referred to the whole of London, but gradually it came to mean the prosperous (usually financial) companies and related organisations based in the square mile covered by the Corporation of the City of London.

More recently still, the City has come to mean the loose cluster of headquarters and main centres of operations for the prosperous, often global (and still usually financial) companies based in central London. The common definition now also includes the major developments at Canary Wharf.

It is this rough definition that we will be working with.

London is currently, along with New York City, the world's leading financial centre, and it has the largest city gross domestic product (GDP) in Europe and the fifth largest in the world.

One of the main features of both the traditional City and Canary Wharf is how few people actually live there, compared with how many people work there every day. The impact of modern technology and the potential for mobile and remote working has reduced the number of people residing in the City over the last decade, but in 2009 (according to Office for National Statistics (ONS) figures) there were only about 11,500 people living in the City of London, and (as at 2012) nearly 317,000 work there – more than 27 times as many. In fact, there are more businesses registered in the City (12,755) than there are people living there. At the last count, 3,095 of these businesses were finance and insurance enterprises.

The City of London contributes 2.4% of the total national income of the UK each year and people working in the City of London have a higher average gross weekly pay than in the rest of the UK, earning £917 compared with £497 in England and Scotland and £453 in Wales (ONS figures April 2012). Of course, this does include the distortion to the average caused by a comparatively small number of people earning enormous wages. Of 376 UK districts covered in the 2001 census, the City also had the largest percentage of employed people and of people who said they had no religious beliefs.

According to the Bank for International Settlements, in 2010 the City was the largest international banking centre in the world, with banks in the UK accounting for over 20% of global cross-border banking business. External lending by banks in the UK to foreign companies and other entities amounted to over $4.5 trillion in December 2010. Total banking assets in the UK, at around £8 billion, are equivalent to more than five times the UK's GDP, or the amount it 'earns' each year.

According to Forbes, 15 of the 40 largest companies in the UK are financial institutions.

Most of the world's largest banks have chosen to locate key parts of their international business activities in the City. There are 241 foreign banks with branches or subsidiaries in the UK, more than in any other country.

To put this all into perspective, here are some facts and figures from October 2012 about the nature and volume of financial business in the City.

- Daily foreign exchange turnover in London is $1.9 trillion or 37% of global activity.[1]
- 19% of the global foreign equity market is traded in London.[2]
- 70% of the global Eurobond turnover is traded in London.[3]
- Over 120 million metal contracts a year are traded in London, with an average daily turnover of $46 billion.[4]
- Nearly 1.3 billion contracts a year are traded on London's International Financial Futures Exchange.[5]
- There is £4.1 trillion in funds under management in the UK.[6]
- Nearly £36 billion trade surplus is generated by the UK financial services sector.[7]
- The City has a 95% share of the EU emissions trading scheme.[8]
- 604 foreign companies are listed on the London Stock Exchange, including the AIM market.[9]
- There are 241 foreign banks in London.[10]
- 19% share of global hedge fund assets are in the UK.[11]
- The City is a leading western centre for Islamic finance, with 22 banks supplying Islamic financial services, five of which are fully Sharia compliant.[12]
- In 2009 the City had a 21% share of the global market in marine insurance, making the UK the world leader.[13]

[1] Bank for International Settlements

[2] TheCityUK

[3] TheCityUK

[4] London Metal Exchange

[5] NYSE Liffe

[6] Investment Management Association

[7] TheCityUK

[8] TheCityUK

[9] London Stock Exchange

[10] TheCityUK

[11] TheCityUK

[12] TheCityUK

[13] TheCityUK

2

Professions in the City: an overview

Each of the sectors we will be looking at has different characteristics, different leading companies, different entrance requirements and different success criteria; moreover, each requires different qualifications, either at the outset or to enable career progress.

We shall look at the following areas:

- banking: retail and commercial; investment
- insurance
- accountancy
- management consultancy.

Banking: a brief history

Interestingly, the development of the processes of banking is thought to be even older than the invention of money, with early deposits made in the form of grain, precious metals or other items that could be stored, traded and transported.

Indeed, the first 'banks' were the merchants who made loans to farmers and traders carrying goods between cities. The first accounts of this can be dated to around 4,000 years ago, in Assyria and Babylonia.

Around 2,000 years later, moneylenders introduced two new practices: accepting deposits, and changing money. There is evidence of this being done by money lenders in Ancient Greece and subsequently across the Roman Empire, with parallel but independent development starting in the ancient realms of China and India.

'Banking' in the more modern sense of the word evolved in Europe throughout the Middle Ages and into the Renaissance, particularly in the prosperous trading city states of Venice, Genoa and Florence. By the 14th century, successful banking families were starting to establish branches away from their home cities to extend their influence and increase their profits. Banking prospered in all major cities, and Queen Elizabeth I opened the City's London Royal Exchange in 1571. At that time moneychangers were already called bankers, but stockbrokers were not allowed in the Royal Exchange because of their rude manners and had to carry out their business in nearby buildings such as coffee houses. Although the description 'a bank' was used to refer to the offices of moneychangers, it did not carry the connotations it does today.

There were also clear and distinct strata of professionals. Bankers who did business with heads of state were at the top, followed by those involved with the city exchanges, and at the bottom were pawn shops, also known as 'Lombards'. Many Lombard streets can be found in European cities, usually having been the site where a prominent pawn shop was located. It was not until the 17th century that there were banking houses in the City of London that carried out their business in a manner similar to today.

During the last century there were significant changes in the way banks worked, enabled by developments in telecoms and computing and leading to huge increases in the successful firms' size and geographic spread. Even so, the financial crisis at the end of the last century saw the failure of several iconic names in banking, adding a note of qualification to the phrase 'too big to fail' that emerged at the same time.

Modern banking is subdivided into many different categories. Most banks are profit-making, some — such as government-run banks — are not, and some are almost speculative, such as community development banks, which are regulated banks that exist to serve emerging or underserved populations or markets. For our purposes we are going to consider banking under three main headings: retail, commercial and investment.

Retail and commercial banking

Definitions

In essence, **retail banking** is when a banking institution deals directly with individuals and small businesses, rather than with corporations of other banks.

Of course, this definition is slightly malleable at the edges. Different retail banks, for example, will deal with different sizes of 'small' business, often determining their eligibility to be handled by their commercial banking arm by the value of banking business done rather than, say, the scale of the enterprise or the number of people it employs. In a similar manner, 'high net worth' individuals will often be customers of 'private banks' (many 'off-shore banks', usually located in countries with low taxation and minimal regulation, are essentially private banks), but this is a niche specialism into which a successful banking career might lead and will be discussed later.

The types of service provided include:

- savings accounts
- transactional accounts
- mortgages
- personal loans
- debit cards
- credit cards.

Commercial banking is similar to retail banking, except that its customers are usually medium to large commercial companies. Most large 'retail' banks will also have either a commercial banking arm or another company within the group to which they will refer commercial clients. Their main business is still receiving deposits from customers and making loans.

The definition came to prominence after the Great Depression, when legislation in the USA (the Glass–Steagall Act of 1933) forcibly divided the business of deposit-taking and loans from capital market businesses, or 'investment banking'.

This separation was felt necessary because of the fundamental conflict of interest which looms when one bank is developing higher-risk financial products and looking for corporate clients to which to sell them, while is also advancing money to corporate clients and advising them of what financial products to buy as investments.

The separation between commercial and investment banking softened more and more during the age of financial liberalisation and globalisation from 1990 to 2007. In 1999 the US government repealed elements of the 1933 Act and introduced new legislation allowing the creation of 'universal banks' (covering both retail/commercial and investment banking) in 1999.

Universal banks have been the model in operation in Europe, but in the wake of the financial crisis, Sir Mervyn King, the Governor of the Bank of England, has strongly urged that separation be made a legal requirement in the UK. This would break up the bigger banks. In 2011, the Independent Commission on Banking published the Vickers Report, which stopped short of requiring separation but advocated 'ring fencing' of UK retail banking services and higher capital requirements. The aim would be, at least in part, to guarantee the safety of private accounts in retail banks in the event of high-risk capital ventures failing. The reality of implementing the proposals in the report is still under discussion.

Leading retail/commercial banks

Many developed economies have a significant number of sizeable, independent local banks, but this is not the case in the UK. The volume of takeovers and mergers during the second half of the 20th century has consolidated the market into a small number of independent players, of whom four are significantly larger than the others. The assets of the smallest of 'the Big Four', in order of market capitalisation, are more than seven times greater than the next ranked bank, Standard Chartered.

The Big Four are: HSBC Holdings plc (HSBC); Royal Bank of Scotland Group plc (RBS); Lloyds Banking Group plc (Lloyds); and Barclays plc (Barclays). Although the head office of RBS is in Edinburgh, it has a significant presence in London, hence its inclusion.

The table below summarises the key facts relating to the Big Four.

TABLE 1: The Big Four

Bank	Head office and website	Employees and global presence	Products	Market value (£bn)*	Assets (£bn)
HSBC	8 Canada Square Canary Wharf London E14 5HQ Tel: 020 7991 8888 Website: www. hsbc.com	• 288,316 employees (as of 2011) • 7,200 offices • 85 countries	• Credit cards • Consumer banking • Corporate banking • Finance and insurance • Investment banking • Mortgage loans • Private banking • Wealth management	122.4	1,736
RBS	36 St Andrew Square Edinburgh EH2 2YB London office: Royal Bank of Scotland plc Head Office 250 Bishopsgate London EC2M 3AA Tel: 020 7085 5000 Website: www.rbs.com	• 150,000 employees (as of 2012) c. 2,300 branches • 40+ countries	• Finance and insurance • Consumer banking • Corporate banking • Investment banking • Global wealth management • Mortgages • Credit cards	49.9	2,508
Lloyds	25 Gresham Street London EC2V 7HN Tel: 020 7626 1500 Website: www. lloydsbankinggroup. com	• 120,499 employees (2011) • 2,940 branches (UK figure) • 30+ countries	• Credit cards • Consumer banking • Corporate banking • Finance and insurance • Investment banking • Mortgage loans • Private banking • Wealth management	44.4	1,195
Barclays	One Churchill Place Canary Wharf London E14 5HP Tel: 020 7116 1000 Website: www. barclays.co.uk	• 146,100 employees (2011) • 4,750 branches • 50+ countries	• Retail banking • Commercial banking • Investment banking • Investment management	38.3	2,320

* Source: Bloomberg.com, as at 24 February 2011.

Notes:

1. The British Government owns 84% of the Royal Bank of Scotland Group's ordinary shares, but the Royal Bank of Scotland remains, officially, independent.

2. The British Government owns 43% of Lloyds Banking Group, but the bank remains officially in the private sector.

Who owns what?

The consolidation of the retail banking sector in the UK is not always apparent from the number of banking 'brands' that are still operating on the high street and on the internet. Here are the other well-known names owned by the Big Four banks.

TABLE 2: Banks owned by the Big Four

Owner	Bank trading name
HSBC	First Direct
RBS	NatWest, Coutts, Royal Bank of Scotland, Ulster Bank
Lloyds	Bank of Scotland, Birmingham Midshires, C&G, Halifax, Lloyds TSB, Intelligent Finance
Barclays	Woolwich Mortgages

The banks run by the British Government are:

- **National Savings and Investments (NS&I)**
- **Northern Rock**
- **Bradford and Bingley (mortgage business).**

You could be forgiven for thinking that the Hongkong and Shanghai Banking Corporation (HSBC) is a foreign-owned company, it is actually British-founded and British-owned, whereas the familiar 'British' retail banking names in Table 3 are all owned by foreign banks.

Despite the dominance of the Big Four in the UK retail banking market, there are still some independent local or specialist banks.

TABLE 3: 'British' banks owned by foreign banks

UK Bank Trading Name	Owner
Clydesdale Bank	National Australia Bank
Egg Banking plc	Citigroup (USA)
Northern Bank	Danske Bank of Denmark
Santander (formerly Abbey, Alliance & Leicester, part of Bradford and Bingley)	Banco Santander (Spain)
Yorkshire Bank	National Australia Bank

The Financial Standards Authority (FSA) keeps a full list, which is updated every month (www.fsa.gov.uk/pubs/list_banks/2012/mar12.pdf).

Careers in retail banking

This is a relatively tough time for retail banks. After 10 years of growth and increasing profits, they now face pressures from both regulatory changes and from their own customers, who want to see the banks made visibly safer and fairer. Despite this, there are still opportunities.

This is a large sector with a great many career paths. The stereotypical career is to join a bank, train as a cashier and move through the levels of management to managing a high street branch. In reality, retail banking incorporates not only branch working, but also online and telephone banking, and all streams usually involve extensive dealings with customers.

It is an attractive option and the larger employers tend to operate graduate training schemes, often built of six-monthly modules during which you gain experience of managing groups of staff in different parts of the organisation – or different companies within the group. However, competition is intense, and students must apply early and are usually expected to have a 2.i degree or better. Successful candidates will also need to be willing to make a long-term commitment to this sort of work – often with a single company for several years, during which they will usually be required to study for specialist or professional qualifications.

A degree is by no means essential for obtaining an entry-level job in retail banking and people often start as bank administrative or clerical staff, cashiers, contact centre operatives and so on. Progression from these positions is entirely possible, based on the flair and hard work of the individual involved, and their ability to demonstrate the accuracy of their work, their reliability, their honesty, and that they can get things done smoothly and with a minimum of fuss, presenting their superiors with solutions more often than problems. The websites of retail banks normally have details of how to make direct applications to them.

"A successful career in retail banking demands a good understanding of the sector and the current challenges it

faces, together with a solid economic background and strong technical and customer relationship skills. "

Dr Barbara Casu, Course Director for the Cass Business School's MSc in Banking and International Finance

The initial pay for graduates is not likely to be high (c. £25,000–£29,000 in 2012), but the reward is getting to take on management responsibility earlier than in many careers. There is also the opportunity to gain experience in different areas, from dealing with customers face to face in branches, to call centre operations and managerial roles. Early roles are about understanding how the operational side of banking works, which can be quite intensive in terms of learning the administrative work involved. A finance-related degree is not always relevant, but highly numerate graduates with strong communications skills will always be attractive.

"A lot of candidates get on a retail graduate scheme, but really want to be in investment — this is ludicrous. You need to pick the biggest players in your chosen sector. It's hard to move from retail to investment these days. "

Soraya Pugh, Head of Graduate Recruitment, FreshMinds Talent (www.freshmindstalent.co.uk)

Most graduate jobs in banking are found in branch management or relationship management, but there are other roles, for example, in marketing and product, risk management and compliance. In the early years of a banking career there is usually the opportunity to move between different streams of work to find what interests you most.

Given the diversity of the field and the size of some of the major employers, there are many career paths possible, but a person joining as a bank cashier might, for example, aim to be promoted as follows:

- Cashier
- Senior Bank Cashier
- Specialist Customer Service Adviser
- Trainee Manager (this is effectively the point to which many retail banking graduate entry schemes will take a new starter)
- Manager.

As well as developing staff management, customer handling and technical skills, a Bank Manager is expected to generate new business for the bank, and to set and achieve targets for different teams under their direction. This means that they will need a thorough knowledge of the bank's (and its competitors') financial products and services, including mortgages, loans, shares, business options and insurance packages. It is possible for a Senior Bank Manager to be in overall charge of one large branch or several smaller branches.

Managers can spend a lot of time out of office, visiting business clients and attending meetings and conferences. They also work closely with local chambers of commerce, development agencies, and other professionals such as solicitors, accountants and estate agents. In some branches there may be a separate Business Manager.

The Branch Manager will also compile, interpret and present management information and reports, both to the staff in the branch and to head office.

Speed of progression is likely to vary. Promotion can be reasonably expected every two or three years, but a lot will depend on ability and aptitude; progression is performance-related. Promotion may be dependent on achieving relevant qualifications and may also mean leaving one branch for another, or for a regional or head office, so mobility is expected if required.

Promotion beyond Bank Manager is likely to be to a regional management position, or specialist roles in head office focusing on, for example:

- business /corporate banking
- finance
- liaison with regulatory bodies such as the FSA (which will soon be split into two bodies, the Financial Conduct Authority (FCA) and the Prudential Regulation Authority (PRA)).
- training
- treasury

'Bank Manager' is a fairly general job title covering a lot of roles, as shown above, and this is reflected in the expected remuneration package. According to National Salary Data, salaries typically range between about £21,500 and £68,500, with bonuses of up to around £30,000 per annum.

Investment banking

Definitions

Investment banks work primarily in higher finance. They help companies and, indeed, governments access the capital markets (such as the stock market or the bond market) to raise money for expansion, mergers and acquisitions (M&A) or for other purposes. For example, if a major UK firm wanted to sell £500 million worth of bonds to build new factories in the Far East, an investment bank would help them find buyers for the bonds and provide teams of lawyers and accountants, as needed, to organise all the paperwork. The industry is heavily concentrated in a small number of major financial centres, including the City of London, New York City, Hong Kong and Tokyo.

Investment banks are typically engaged in the following types of activity.

- **Raising equity capital**, e.g. helping to launch the first sale of stock by a private company to the public (an Initial Public Offering or IPO), or creating a special class of preferred stock that can be placed with sophisticated investors such as insurance companies or banks.
- **Raising debt capital**, e.g. issuing bonds to help raise money for a business expansion as outlined above.
- **Insuring bonds or launching new products**, such as setting up a credit default swap (CDS). This means that the seller of the CDS will compensate the buyer in the event of a loan default.
- **Proprietary trading**, where teams of specialist in-house traders (who do not deal with clients) invest or trade the investment bank's own money for its private account. For example, the investment bank may believe that the price of gold will rise, so they speculate in gold futures, acquire call options on gold mining firms, or purchase gold bullion outright for storage in secure vaults.

The **buy side** and the **sell side** are the two main dimensions in investment banking.

The sell side usually refers to selling shares of new IPOs, placing new bond issues, market making (setting the buying and selling prices for different financial instruments), or helping clients make transactions successfully. In general, they are creating and selling some form of financial product or service.

The buy side, as the name implies, is the other side of the coin. This involves working with pension funds, mutual funds, hedge funds and those wishing to invest, by advising them how to maximise their return when trading or investing in stocks, bonds or other securities.

There are investment banks which specialise in one or the other of these sides, but they can both be found in the larger financial institutions.

'Front', 'middle' and 'back' office services are the traditional divides in an investment bank.

Front office services are seen as the most glamorous element of the business. Typical activities include:

- investment management for institutions or high net worth individuals
- merchant banking: the bank puts money into privately owned firms in exchange for levels of share ownership, and offers advice on management and strategy
- support for major M&A activity, for example negotiating on behalf of the client with the target company
- capital market and investment research reports, prepared by in-house analysts either for internal use or for sale to selected clients
- strategy development, including risk limits and the parameters for asset allocation, often work done for internal as well as external clients
- researching companies and preparing reports on then, often using 'buy' or 'sell' ratings. This does not directly generate income but helps guide the activity of the traders, inform the advice of the sales force, and the investment bankers in covering their clients. These services can also be made available to clients for specific projects. Because there is a potential conflict of interest, as published analysis could affect the bank's profits, this relationship is highly regulated, with a Chinese wall between public and private functions
- sales: a sales force will maintain relationships with corporations or high-value individual clients so that they can call on them to suggest trading ideas and take orders. These orders are relayed to the appropriate trading desks to price and carry out the trades or to develop new products to fit an identified need

- corporate finance, including the issue of 'commercial paper' to cover clients' short-term needs for money. This is done by the bank selling promissory notes on behalf of their clients, at a discount on their face value, with the promise that client firm will buy them back at a set date, this promise being guaranteed by the bank.

Corporate finance, or 'investment banking divisions' (IBDs) are generally divided into two groups: industry coverage and product coverage. Industry coverage groups focus on a particular industry or market sector such as technology, healthcare or manufacturing, and maintain and develop contacts and relationships within this sector in order to build business for the bank. Product coverage groups focus on certain types of financial products, such as M&A, public finance, asset finance and leasing, equity and high-grade debt. The two groups assemble complementary teams to meet the exact needs of major clients for specific projects.

Middle office services are still seen internally as quite high status, but less so than front office services. Typical activities include:

- corporate treasury, which is responsible for an investment bank's funding, capital structure and management, and liquidity risk monitoring
- financial control, which monitors capital flow, evaluates the levels of money coming in and going out of the bank against the liquidity levels required and reduces the buying and trading volumes available to the other services to keep the bank within safe parameters. Corporate strategy often falls under this heading.

Back office services are often considered to be much lower status and, indeed, are sometimes outsourced to specialist companies. That said, the reality is that these services enable the whole enterprise to function. Back office functions include:

- information technology department – overseeing the software and hardware that traders use for their work to make sure it is up to date, fit for purpose and functioning as needed
- confirming trades by checking that the correct securities are bought, are sold and are settled for the correct amounts
- creating new trading algorithms that may trigger sales and purchasing activity by traders

The illustration below shows a model of a full-service investment bank, although each of the primary divisions shown may have many specialised sub-divisions within it.

FIGURE 1: Functional design of a full-service investment bank

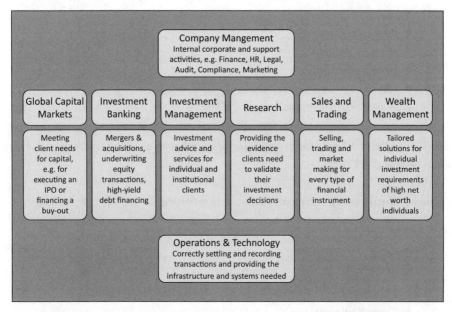

- compliance – ensuring that the bank complies with the different government regulations and restrictions as they apply, for example to investment banks and insurance companies.

Leading investment banks

Investment banking is a more global business than retail banking and staff may have to work anywhere they are needed: the more senior the position, the more likely this is to happen. This is primarily a business of relationships and you need to go where the clients and targets are.

The following are the largest full-service global investment banks (collectively known as 'bulge bracket' banks), offering clients both advisory and financial banking services, plus sales, market making and research:

- Bank of America
- Barclays Capital

- BNP Paribas
- Citigroup
- Credit Suisse
- Deutsche Bank
- Goldman Sachs
- JPMorgan Chase
- Morgan Stanley
- Nomura Securities
- UBS
- Wells Fargo Securities.

Details of the most popular of the bulge bracket banks, as voted for by graduates, can be found in Chapter 5.

Large financial service companies combine retail and/or commercial banking with investment banking and often insurance services. These are the largest of this type of organisation. The name of the 'parent' bank appears first, followed by the name of the investment banking firm in brackets, if this is noticeably different:

- ABN AMRO
- Banco Santander
- Bank of China (BOC International Holdings)
- Bank of Communications (BOCOM International Holdings)
- Bank of Montreal (BMO Capital Markets)
- BBVA
- BB&T (BB&T Capital Markets)
- Canadian Imperial Bank of Commerce (CIBC World Markets)
- China Construction Bank (CCB International Holdings)
- Commerzbank (Dresdner Kleinwort, Eurohypo)
- CréditAgricole
- Daiwa Securities
- DBS Bank (Capital Markets Group)
- HSBC
- ING Group
- İş Bankası (Is Investment)
- KBC Bank
- KeyCorp (KeyBanc Capital Markets)
- Kotak Mahindra Bank

- Lloyds Banking Group (Lloyds Bank Wholesale Banking & Markets)
- Macquarie Group
- Mizuho Financial Group
- Monte deiPaschi di Siena (MPS Finance)
- M&T Bank
- Natixis
- Nomura Holdings
- PNC Financial Services (Harris Williams & Company)
- Rabobank
- Royal Bank of Canada (RBC Capital Markets)
- Royal Bank of Scotland (RBS GBM)
- Sanlam (Sanlam)
- Sberbank
- Scotiabank (Scotia Capital)
- SociétéGénérale (SG CIB)
- Standard Bank
- Standard Chartered Bank
- State Bank of India (SBI Capital Markets)
- Stifel Financial (StifelNicolaus)
- SunTrust (Robinson Humphrey)
- Toronto-Dominion Bank (TD Securities)
- UniCredit (UBM).

The following are the most notable **independent investment banks and large cap advisory firms** that are not connected with retail/commercial banks. They offer M&A advice, brokerage services and underwriting of securities:

- Allen & Company
- BBY Ltd
- Brown, Shipley & Co.
- Cain Brothers
- Cantor Fitzgerald
- Capstone Partners
- Centerview Partners
- China International Capital Corporation
- CITIC Securities
- Close Brothers Group
- CLSA

- Collins Stewart Hawkpoint
- Corporate Finance Associates
- Cowen Group
- C.W. Downer & Co.
- Daewoo Securities
- Defoe Fournier & Cie.
- Duff & Phelps
- Europa Partners
- FBR Capital Markets
- Financo
- Foros Group
- Gleacher & Co.
- Guggenheim Partners
- Guosen Securities
- Imperial Capital
- Investec
- Investment Technology Group
- Jefferies & Co.
- Keefe, Bruyette & Woods
- Ladenburg Thalmann
- Lazard
- Lincoln International
- Marathon Capital
- Mediobanca
- Miller Buckfire & Co.
- M.M.Warburg & CO
- Moelis & Company
- Morgan Keegan & Company
- N M Rothschild & Sons
- Needham and Company
- Newedge
- Oppenheimer & Co.
- Panmure Gordon
- Park Lane
- Pottinger (Australia)
- Raymond James
- Robert W. Baird & Company
- Sagent Advisors

- Sandler O'Neill + Partners
- Sanford Bernstein
- Stephens Inc.
- Vermilion Partners
- Wedbush Securities
- WR Hambrecht + Co.

There are also about a thousand **specialist boutique investment banks** in the major financial centres. They are a good alternative entry point to investment banking if you are not successful in getting a position with one of the bulge bracket firms, and they are also less sensitive to poorer academic records. (By 'poorer', we still mean 'very good', but perhaps not a first class honours degree from Oxford.) A list of those working in London, with contact details, can be found in Appendix 1.

Careers in investment banking

There is no set career path or career progression in investment banking. Arrangements vary between banks and the rate of progression will be different for different people. Pay is also largely individual, depending on the service line where you work, your performance and how much money you bring in. Bonuses will also depend on both achievement and the seniority of the person involved.

As described above, there are a large number of specialist areas in investment banking, but most new graduates who are successful obtaining a job with a major firm will have done so through a graduate entry scheme or an internship (paid or unpaid).

The names of the different levels vary between banks, but a 'typical' structure would be:

- Analyst
- Associate
- Assistant Vice President (AVP)/Vice President (VP)/Director/Executive Director
- Managing Director
- Partner.

We will look at each of these, but with particular emphasis on the first two steps.

Analyst

The most common role for a new graduate is to join as an Analyst on a two- or three-year programme. An Analyst will usually work with an Associate, supporting them in their work with clients. It is unlikely that an Analyst would be called on to speak at a client meeting, or to get involved in major commitments or decisions, but it can happen. Since this is the lowest rung on the professional ladder, the job entails long hours and a lot of what has been described as 'grunt work'.

At the end of the two-year programme most Analysts will leave, either to pursue other opportunities such as studying to become a Chartered Financial Analyst (CFA), or to return to university to do an MBA before returning to investment banking. A lot depends on the policy of each firm: some tend to let all their Analysts go, but many recognise that it is sensible to retain people who have already proved to be valuable assets for the firm. The CFA usually means a change in direction away from investment banking and into investment companies and mutual funds or consultancy, government regulation or academia, as, for example, Portfolio Managers or Research Analysts. According to the CFA Institute, only about 16% of qualifying CFAs go back into investment banking. At the end of the first three years, most Analysts who have not been promoted will leave the bank.

When investment banks are recruiting for Associates from an MBA programme, those with previous experience as an Analyst will be at a significant advantage, particularly if their experience is with one of the bulge bracket firms. One Oxford economics graduate, accepted to Goldman Sachs' graduate traineeship, said on efinancialnews.com:

> *"I feel like I may have sold my soul. Don't expect to see me for the next two years. On the upside it will look impressive on my CV."*

Associate

An Associate is normally either a newly graduated MBA or, more probably, an Analyst who has been promoted after three to four years with the firm.

The expectation is that you will normally be an Associate for about another three years. It is still a fairly junior position with a lots of hard and basic work, but slightly fewer hours than an Analyst (reportedly around 70 hours a week). You may be paired with an Analyst reporting to you on specific projects.

However, the difference is that you are now 'in' and this is the chance to prove that you have what it takes to be successful. If you can show your technical skills and leadership abilities, add value to transactions or prove your value to the firm through other routes, your bonus may be considerable and you may be on your way to the next step up.

The exact duties of an Associate will vary according to the different requirements of different banks, but there is a general skill set and three specific skill sets relating to the different banking areas:

- investment banking, corporate finance and M&A
- debt and equity capital markets
- sales and trading positions.

Assistant Vice President (AVP)/Vice President (VP)/Director/ Executive Director

The name can vary and there are gradations within this level of seniority, but this is the next step up after working as an Associate. A successful employee is usually promoted to this level after three years or so. It is also quite routine for Associates who are not going to be promoted to leave the firm at this point. This promotion is highly competitive. For convenience, we will refer to this level as VP.

Occasionally, senior managers from a target market sector can be brought in at this level, particularly in business development roles. For example, experienced senior M&A managers at British Telecom might be recruited for the Telecom M&A team in a major bank.

The role of the VP is often to be the day-to-day project manager on major deals that a Managing Director has struck with a client. The VP will 'execute' the deal – in other words, they will make it happen. The VP will act as the main contact with the client while directing the work of any Associates and Analysts on the project. They will plan out the project, determining what tasks have to be completed and by when, and assigning resources to accomplish this. If this is an M&A project, the VP will also be the main contact with the potential target firm or firms, as well as the accountants, lawyers, financial regulators, internal compliance teams, co-advisers and any other relevant parties.

The VP also has to begin generating his or her own business. A VP is likely to be allocated a portfolio of clients, with whom they will need to meet regularly and to whom they will be expected to pitch ideas. They will accompany the Managing Director to meetings with major clients, and meet alone with less important clients. The work becomes far more about co-ordination and relationships than it is about technical work, and most of their time will be spent in client meetings, on the phone or writing emails.

Since they are given more autonomy in their work and are judged on results, a VP's working hours can be significantly lower than those of an Analyst or an Associate, depending on how well they get the work done through others. Also, while their time in the office may drop to 50 or 60 hours a week, there is also an unspoken requirement that they remain available to clients during evenings and weekends.

Managing Director (MD)

Once again, promotion to this level is extremely competitive and many VPs do not achieve it. There is no set timescale for this step up, although it is usual for someone on the rise to spend perhaps three years as a VP, then another two or three years as a Senior VP or Director before being considered for promotion to MD. Once promoted, there is generally no limit to the time an employee can spend as MD and no guarantee of progression to Partner.

The role is similar to that of a Senior VP, but involves relationships with higher-value clients and often very much bigger deals. The MD will take the lead in, for example, major M&A work, including negotiating the fees for the assignment, determining the strategy for the project, all senior-level client meetings and so on. They will also manage their own teams, setting their strategies and overseeing their business development activities and resulting deals.

MDs will liaise with senior management through the bank, such the Head of Investment Banking, Country Heads and other MDs of other geographic or sector teams. The role of the MD is not just to generate fees for their own department, but to assist with selling all the products of the bank, for which they will receive recognition and a proportion of the credit.

In a large firm it is possible for MDs to progress to become team leaders, country or product heads, but many are content to stay at this level for many years. At this level, multi-million-pound bonuses are not unknown, depending on the level of fees generated by the MD.

Partner/CEO

The top of the tree; but in reality, there are often more levels and gradations of Partner than there are in the posts leading up to this level. Sometimes the top management levels of the organisation may be restricted to Partners; in other banks, it may be possible that partnership is a status and remuneration arrangement for someone in a type of role that can also be carried out by a very senior employee.

Insurance

A brief history

One of the first formal systems of insurance known is the Babylonian Code of Hammurabi, which dates from around 1750 BC, and applied to early Mediterranean sailing merchants. It allowed a merchant to pay an additional premium to a lender from whom he had taken a loan to fund his voyage. This was in exchange for the lender cancelling the loan if the vessel and cargo were lost at sea.

It is thought that insurance, in a more modern form, has been around since medieval times, possibly earlier. In Europe, there is evidence of insurance being formalised (through a contract) as early as 1347, and it is thought that at this time marine insurance was commonplace among all the maritime nations of Europe.

In London, insurance developed greatly throughout the 17th and 18th centuries, when merchants and traders would meet at Lloyd's to do business and underwrite risks associated with shipping. These individuals would consider the total value of a ship and its cargo as outlined in a formal document, which they then signed, indicating how much of the risk they were prepared to cover. If nothing happened to the ship, the underwriter would keep a premium. If the ship and its cargo were lost, the underwriter would pay up. By the end of the 18th century the first companies specialising in insurance had been established.

The principles of insurance have not really changed since that time, but the items being insured have changed dramatically. It is now possible to buy insurance for almost anything, with different firms specialising in different types of risk. Today there are two main types of insurance market.

1. The **wholesale market** focuses mainly on the London market. This includes a number of UK and international insurance companies operating in London as well as the syndicates of Lloyd's of London. These companies and syndicates will normally share risks, placed in the market by specialist brokers, which are often very large and sometimes a little unusual.

2. The **retail market** deals with individuals' insurance needs, such as home, car and travel insurance. This market also covers pensions and life cover.

The insurance industry today

According to the Association of British Insurers, in 2011 the UK insurance industry was the third largest in the world, managing investments equating to over a quarter of the net worth of the UK economy and paying around £10.4 billion in taxes to the government each year.

According to the ONS, the industry employs around 290,000 people in the UK (more than 25% of all jobs in the financial services) and earns 28% of its income (£56 billion) from premiums from overseas businesses.

Almost every adult and every business has some form of insurance:

- 19.6 million households have contents insurance
- 16.5 million have buildings insurance
- 24.3 million private vehicles are insured

- 4.4 million commercial vehicles are insured
- 8.5 million households have long-term insurance products
- 29.6 million people have life assurance policies.

There are 1,005 insurance companies in the UK carrying out general insurance business (such as commercial, motor vehicle, health and household insurance). Of these, 411 are registered in the UK and authorised by the FSA. The other 594 are registered elsewhere in the EU. They are all authorised by the European Economic Area (EEA) and are allowed to open branches here and transact business under the supervision of the member state where the company is registered. This is known as 'passporting' into the UK under the Third Non-Life Insurance Directive.

There are 309 businesses allowed to carry out long-term business (including pensions, investments and life insurance), of which 129 are registered in the UK and authorised by the FSA. The other 180 are EEA authorised and passporting into the UK under the Third Non-Life Insurance Directive.

The top 10 general insurance groups account for 67% of that sector and the top 10 life and pensions groups account for 79% of that sector.

Careers in insurance

There are three main employment sectors in insurance:

- the London market
- insurance companies
- insurance brokers.

All areas overlap in the London market and employers here will be insurance companies, reinsurance companies, national insurance broking houses and underwriting syndicates (such as Lloyd's of London). In these businesses, the roles open to graduates are Underwriter, Insurance Broker, Risk Analyst, Claims Inspector, Loss Adjuster, Investment Fund Manager and roles in reinsurance.

The London market

The London market is a distinct and separate part of the insurance industry that is centred in the City of London and developed from those early deals at Lloyd's coffee shop in the 17th century. All of the world's 20 largest reinsurance groups are represented here and the focus is on internationally traded insurance and reinsurance. There is also an emphasis on high-exposure risks. Insurance in the City is a truly global sector, and the number and range of players in this market means that this is a vibrant and exciting place to work in insurance.

Lloyd's of London

Lloyd's does not operate as an insurance company or a bank, but rather as a market whose members form syndicates to insure risks. Each syndicate is run by a Managing Agent and staffed by Underwriters, and is usually backed by capital from corporate sources and some funding from individual members. The syndicates write a vast range of policies in insurance and reinsurance. There are over 80 syndicates at Lloyd's and 50 Managing Agents offering specialist underwriting to clients in over 200 countries and territories. Business here is conducted face to face between insurance brokers (representing the client) and underwriters (working for the syndicates).

Insurance Underwriter

Underwriters assess the level of risk that needs to be covered and decide whether cover should be offered. They set the terms for insurance policies and decide how much should be charged for the cover. The skill of the Underwriter lies in pricing the policy at a level that is still competitive for the client but high enough to cover any potential claims and make a profit for the business.

The work involves gathering as much background information as possible about the risk and studying the insurance proposals. Specialist risk assessments may also need to be commissioned from experts such as surveyors, and that information is used in the preparation of quotes and policies for clients. An Underwriter may also be involved in negotiating terms with a Broker or directly with the client.

Underwriters work for all types of insurance company, including Lloyd's of London. Sound judgement and an enquiring mind, along with numeracy, communication and decision-making skills, are all vital to be successful as an Underwriter. A good reputation and strong contacts can also be important in securing business, as can a background in law, economics, business studies, science or engineering.

Insurance Broker

Brokers work independently of insurance companies and act as intermediaries between the client (seeking insurance) and the insurer. They need to register to act and can specialise in particular areas of insurance. Brokers need to be good at building close relationships with clients and Underwriters and will need to generate their own business.

Insurance Claims Inspector

Once an insurance claim is submitted, it is up to the Claims Inspector to decide whether the claim is valid or whether it needs to be investigated. Decisions are usually based on an analysis of the facts at hand and sound judgement. Claims Inspectors also need to have good communication skills to keep all parties involved updated on the progress of the claim. Complex claims will often be passed on to a Loss Adjuster, with the Claims Inspector concentrating on the more straightforward cases. Claims Inspectors normally have many years of experience working in claims.

Insurance Loss Adjuster

When a complex claim that cannot be resolved by the Claims Inspector is submitted, it may be passed to a Loss Adjuster, who will investigate the claim. Loss Adjusters need to be able to gather information and interview the people involved in the events leading to the claim. Good written skills are also important, as they need to produce comprehensive reports, and a technical and analytical mind is essential to decipher all the facts and come to a recommendation for the claim.

Insurance Risk Analyst

Risk Analysts can be found in a range of sectors, not just insurance. In the insurance industry they use statistical tools and research methods to analyse risk and make recommendations on how to minimise and control that risk. Analytical and numeracy skills are essential for this role, as is a good understanding of the industry and issues relating to risk. Many entrants to this profession will have a postgraduate qualification in risk management.

Case study

Olivia Bromley, Cert CII, Aspen

What is your role?

I have just entered the final year of the Aspen Graduate programme, undertaking rotations in different departments, including Underwriting, Claims and Internal Audit.

What were you doing before this?

I graduated from Lancaster University in Law and Spanish – originally I thought I wanted to enter the legal profession.

What do you do in a typical day?

The work is extremely varied. In underwriting I work alongside experienced Underwriters, honing my commercial acumen to evaluate risks presented by brokers, deciding whether, and on what terms, to accept a risk. My most recent rotation, Internal Audit, involved identifying key risks to the business and testing the controls in place over them.

What do you enjoy most about your job?

I am a people person and working in a relationship-based profession lets me employ these skills daily. Being exposed to many different teams, lawyers, experts and brokers, you gain crucial insights into the dynamics of relationships and how these are leveraged to achieve results.

To be a successful Underwriter I must combine logic with complex technical and financial knowledge. I am very intellectually driven, relishing the many opportunities I have to learn from the great minds around me. Longer term, I am excited about the prospect of delivering insurance solutions that positively impact not just Aspen's bottom line but the clients we serve and value.

What is the most challenging part of your role?

Consistently delivering absolute accuracy, numeracy and common sense when under pressure and often to tight deadlines. It's crucial to understand the differing styles of those around you. I am in awe of seasoned Underwriters who are able to articulate what are often complex issues in a clear, concise way.

What skills do you need to be successful in your role?

- Commercial acumen
- People skills
- Communication
- Negotiation
- Analytical thinking
- Drive.

Have you got professional qualifications?

Having gained my CII Certificate in Insurance (Cert CII), I am now working towards my Diploma.

What are the main benefits of working in risk?

You work in a high-performing and dynamic environment, whilst at the same contributing something necessary to the economy and thus society as a whole. There is a deeply ingrained social aspect to the sector and, contrary to many professions in the City, you find excellent rewards with a good work–life balance.

Why did you choose a career in insurance?

One of my professors suggested insurance an alternative career to law, as I could employ many of the aptitudes that I had established whilst studying for my degree. A year into my career I am pleased to say that I would absolutely make the same choice again.

To find out more about this profession, email discover@cii.co.uk

Organisation profile: CII's Discover Risk campaign

London 2012; tsunamis and floods in Asia; riots and flooding in the UK; piracy off the African coast; and an American footballer's hair. These are all linked by insurance.

Called 'the DNA of capitalism', insurance is about managing risks, wherever they may be and however large the sums involved. When disaster strikes, insurance is about restoring a person, a community or a business to the place it held before that disaster.

Recent years have seen our profession stand firm in the face of difficult economic conditions. While big companies in other sectors have collapsed, there have been no major business failures in insurance and companies are maintaining good levels of recruitment for school leavers and graduates.

London occupies a unique position in finance. In our sector, it is the world's leading insurance and reinsurance hub, and the London market is the only place in the world where special risks are underwritten by experienced professionals. These special risks range from coffee tasters' taste buds to guitar players' fingers to complex satellite equipment.

Insurance (or risk, as some people call it) is a people profession. If you are at university, or planning to go there, the best way to build your network is by becoming a Discover member. For a small sum, you can attend networking events with people who already work in the sector, through the CII's national network of practitioners. So, whether you're in London or Belfast, Swansea or Dundee, you're never far from your network.

The CII is the world's largest professional body for insurance, risk and financial services. There are 110,000 CII members in more than 150 countries around the world. In the UK alone there are more than 275,000 people working in our profession, and the sector contributes more than £10 billion in taxes to the government.

If you're a graduate, look for companies offering structured graduate schemes. These schemes will have a professional qualification built in to them. For many, this will be the CII's Advanced Diploma in Insurance, also known as the ACII. This is the most widely recognised qualification and designation in the world of insurance and risk, and is rather like having a passport for your career.

Taking between two and four years, the ACII covers a wide range of subjects, including marketing, economics and law, as well as the technical areas such as risk management, underwriting and broking.

If you're looking at joining straight after school or college, more companies are taking on Apprentices who can get qualified while they earn. It's a smart way to gain experience and avoid university debt.

To find out more about this fascinating and surprising profession, email discover@cii.co.uk.

Accountancy

This section deals with a brief history of accountancy, identifies the most significant 'public practice' firms in the City (independent accountancy firms offering professional services) and outlines some of the key roles in them. For a more detailed, in-depth analysis of working in all aspects of accounting, read *Working in Accountancy* by Sherridan Hughes and Natalie Sermon, published by Trotman.

A brief history

Perhaps not surprisingly, accounting probably pre-dates both the invention of money and the earliest banks. The earliest accounting records date from around 7,000 years ago in Mesopotamia and are records, kept for individuals' use, of numbers of sheep or cattle, volumes of crops and so on.

The evolution of the discipline mirrored the development and growth of the banks and the financial institutions described earlier. The best known accountancy technique, double entry bookkeeping, emerged in northern Italy in the 14th century. The emergence of companies in which people could buy stocks stimulated an interest in mechanisms by which a potential investor, with no hands-on understanding or knowledge of the specific business involved, might assess the risk and profit of an investment. This knowledge was derived from the businesses' accounts.

This led to the development of three specialist roles for accountants.

1. Internal to a business: preparing the accounts.

2. Internal to a business: checking the probity and accuracy of accounts and the general compliance with regulations and legislation; in other words, the auditors (usually only in larger organisations).

3. External to a business: providing an impartial, expert stamp of approval on figures and records produced.

Accountancy is referred to as 'the language of business' and is defined as the communication of financial information about a business to interested parties such as managers and shareholders. The communication is generally in the form of financial statements that show, in monetary terms, the economic resources under the control of management. The 'art' of accountancy is to select reliable, relevant and accurate information and present it in the most user-friendly manner.

The 'Big Four' public practice firms

There are currently around 5,000 public practice firms in the UK, which are mainly accounting firms offering audit, professional and consultancy services. Their clients are public sector bodies, limited and private companies. The primary services offered include audit, tax and advisory. This latter category encompasses everything that is not related to tax and audit, including mergers and acquisitions, corporate finance, performance improvement and risk.

The largest of the public practice firms are known as the 'Big Four' and they are:

- PwC (officially PricewaterhouseCoopers)
- Deloitte (officially Deloitte Touche Tohmatsu Limited)
- Ernst & Young
- KPMG.

In reality, each of these is a network of global firms, which share a common name, brand and quality standards, and which is co-ordinated by a central body, although that central body does not itself practise accountancy or control the firm. Between them these four giants undertake the vast majority of audits for publicly traded and large private companies and for public sector organisations in the UK.

Accountancy is one of the 'classic' graduate careers, and the Big Four accounting firms take on more new graduates every year than almost any other group of employers. Joining one of these firms will usually lead to experience of a wide range of businesses, a professional qualification and the 'credibility stamp' of a Big Four brand on your CV.

However, while this can be a great way to start a career in accounting, there is no denying that it is hard work, with long hours, a lot of basic number crunching at the start and tough exams to pass. As with most of the careers in this book, if you don't do your research first, and then find yourself in a position you aren't enjoying, life will be very hard until you can change things.

Between them, the big firms employ around 47,000 Accountants, which equates to approximately 64% of all the Accountants in public practice organisations in the UK. This only leaves 27,000 working in all the middle-tier firms, high street practices and as sole traders.

There are some impressive large firms in the middle tier (such as BDO and Grant Thornton), but their prospects for major expansion are limited by the fact that all but one of the FTSE 100 companies and 96% of the FTSE 250 are said to be audited by one of the Big Four firms. These firms are probably the most expensive, but they have a substantial reputation.

In the early days of IT, it was said that 'No-one ever got sacked for buying IBM'. In the modern procurement of external audit, 'No-one ever got sacked for buying from the Big Four', although it has led to considerable debate over the apparent power of this audit oligopoly.

Table 4 summarises the key facts relating to the Big Four.

TABLE 4: The 'Big Four' accountancy firms

Firm	UK Head Office and Website	Employees and Global Presence	UK Employees and Offices	Global Revenues ($bn)	UK Revenues (£bn)
PwC	1 Embankment Place London WC2N 6RH Tel: 020 7583 5000 Website: www.pwc. com	• 169,000 staff • 771 offices • in 158 countries	• 845 partners • 16,000 staff • 2,670 trainees • 40 offices	29.2[1]	2.3
Deloitte	Stonecutter Court 1 Stonecutter Street London EC4A 3TR Tel: 020 7936 3000 Website: www. deloitte.com	• 182,000 staff • in 150 countries	• 681 partners • 11,400 staff • 2,020 trainees • 21 offices	28.8[2]	2.0
Ernst & Young	Becket House 1 Lambeth Palace Road London SE1 7EU Tel: 020 7951 2000 Website: www.ey.com	• 152,000 staff • 695 offices • in 140 countries	• 533 partners • 8,400 staff • 1,328 trainees • 21 offices	22.9[3]	1.4
KPMG	Salisbury Square House 8 Salisbury Square London EC4Y 8BB Tel: 020 7311 1000 Website: www. kpmgcareers.co.uk	• 145,000 staff • in 152 countries	• 545 partners • 10,500 staff • 2,088 trainees • 22 offices	22.7[4]	1.6

[1] Source: www.pwc.com (as at 2011)
[2] Source: www.deloitte.com (as at 2011)
[3] Source: www.doingbusiness.ro (as at December 2011)
[4] Source: www.theaustralian.com.au (as at 2011)

PwC

The firm's business in the UK is divided into three main service lines:

1. assurance

2. tax advisory

3. advisory.

And into four main industry specialisms:

1. consumer and industrial products and services

2. financial services

3. technology, communications and entertainment

4. infrastructure, government and utilities.

The firm has worked hard to get a number of regular awards for technical proficiency and for being a 'good corporate citizen'. It regularly features as an outstanding employer of new graduates, has an active community giving programme and has an admirable track record on sustainability and green issues, from thought leadership to actual reductions of CO_2 emissions year on year.

It is seen in the industry as rather bureaucratic and corporate, with little chance of flexibility in promotion in the first four years. There have also been some reports from staff that salary may be in part dependent on how well your division does, and the 'visibility' of your clients, rather than purely on individual effort and achievement. However, this is a feature of a large number of salary and bonus schemes and such reports must always be taken with a pinch of salt. On the other side of the coin, it has a diverse workforce and a good reputation for opportunities for women. It has a largely formal but occasionally 'smart casual' dress code.

Deloitte

In 2010, Deloitte edged ahead of PwC to become the largest professional services group in the world. The full title of the company is Deloitte Touche Tohmatsu (DTTL) and it is a private company established in the UK.

The firm's business in the UK is divided into five main service lines:

1. audit and enterprise risk

2. consulting

3. financial advisory (e.g. corporate finance, insolvency and forensics)

4. tax

5. other (e.g. international financial reporting).

Like PwC, it works hard to achieve both professional and 'good citizenship' awards, and its dedication to diversity has been seen in measures such as the establishment of its Global Retention and Advancement of Women Council, the Global Diversity and Inclusion Community of Practice and its recognition of International Women's Day. In 2010, Deloitte was recognised in the Workingmums.co.uk top employer awards for having the best flexible working and family-friendly policies.

In the industry, Deloitte is recognised as having a friendly and practical 'work hard, play hard' culture that places emphasis on team working and team spirit, with good two-way communication encouraged and achieved. In contrast, day-to-day working life at Deloitte may not actually be as diverse as in other firms. Like PwC, the firm is thought to be rather arrogant. On the other hand, in firms where 'only the best' are recruited to a competitive environment and their job is to be better than their competitors at what they do, it would be surprising if an element of arrogance did not creep in. In terms of City culture, and for the same reasons, this charge could certainly also be levelled at investment banks and management consultants, for example.

There are said to be good prospects for earlier promotion, but training may need to be requested rather than just automatically received. The salaries are said to be good, with good benefits, including interest-free loans, payment of relocation expenses and private gym access.

Ernst & Young

The firm's business in the UK is divided into four main service lines:

1. assurance

2. advisory (actuarial, IT risk, assurance risk and performance improvement)

3. taxation

4. transaction advisory.

Ernst & Young have a good track record of professional awards, winning three times at the Scottish Accountancy Awards and winning two Management Consultancies Association Awards, for Public Sector Outsourcing and Change Management. The firm also has a good reputation in terms of corporate finance.

Ernst & Young has also been recognised for its commitment to corporate social responsibility (CSR), with three Business in the Community Awards for Excellence. In addition, it has a long-standing reputation as a supporter of the arts, sponsoring gallery and museum exhibitions as well as the highly regarded Entrepreneurs of the Year awards and educational programme for children, and assisting with fundraising for the Prince's Trust.

The general impression in the industry is that the culture of Ernst & Young is particularly friendly and liberal, promoting a relaxed, supportive and open climate. The offices are all open plan and not even partners have their own offices. However, 'hot-desking' can easily mean that you sit at a different desk with different neighbours almost every day. The workforce is roughly 50/50 male/female, there are options to work flexibly and it is a moderately flat hierarchy, but the salaries may be a little lower than at the other three major firms.

Ernst & Young is believed to favour the Institute of Chartered Accountants in Scotland (ICAS) qualification, which builds technical competence quickly, and which in turn can help accelerate promotion to middle management earlier than at some of the other firms. There are genuine opportunities for working internationally.

KPMG

The firm's business in the UK is divided into four main service lines:

1. audit

2. tax (business and personal)

3. advisory (transaction, corporate finance, risk, forensic, IT, restructuring and performance)

4. other (that is, business with China).

KPMG has a very good reputation for audit, and has received awards for both technical excellence and for its people. The firm regularly appears in the top 10 of the *Sunday Times* 'Best Big Companies to Work For', winning a special 'lifetime achievement' award for this in 2009 and, in 2011, being ranked higher in this list than any of the other Big Four firms. The same year KPMG was also named 'World's Best Outsourcing Advisers'.

In terms of training and development, KPMG is the only one of the Big Four to have a full-time Professional Qualifications Training team of 17 staff to help and support graduates through their training – support made more practical by the fact that most of the team have studied for the qualifications themselves.

As with the other firms, KPMG have been making efforts to improve their CSR and green credentials over recent years, in particular by allowing their staff to volunteer a half day of their time in their local community each month. Remote working has been actively implemented, increasing the potential for flexibility in working arrangements and salaries are thought to be 'highly competitive'. That said, in 2012, the firm announced that it will not in future be 'exercising its discretion' by paying bonuses to second-year audit trainees who pass their exams first time (usually 80% of them). These bonuses were usually around £1,000, and will apparently save the firm around £400,000. This brings the firm into line with the other major accountancy practices.

Careers in accountancy

The core organisational structure of each of the Big Four firms is very similar. There are variations and the numbers in each category vary, but they tend to be pyramidal. In some of the mid-level organisations, there may also be specialist roles: for example, a person may be paid at an equivalent rate to, say, a Principal, but is not in the hierarchy of command and not in line for consideration for partner. A generic example is shown in Figure 2. Specific projects, client assignments, divisions and departments all tend to follow this basic design, with different numbers in each layer according to scale.

In general, promotion through the ranks depends on achievement, chargeability levels and fees earned. That said, the balance shifts more towards sales as you progress up the structure. It has often been observed at the big firms that

FIGURE 2: Organisational structure in the Big Four accountancy firms

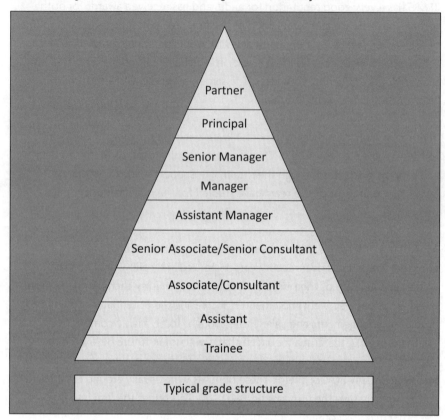

the people best at sales will make Principal and often Partner, but that is not necessarily a reflection of their internal staff or project management skills.

Partnership is of course an 'invitation to join', rather than an 'employee promotion', as the existing Partners offer new Partners the opportunity to buy a stake as a part owner of the firm. This means that there will be 'political' considerations, as well as performance and commercial ones, at play in determining who is invited.

Trainee/Assistant Accountant

"I most enjoy working with different teams — being sociable with those teams during working hours makes the whole job

more enjoyable, but I sometimes get put under unnecessary pressure when other people are free due to strange resourcing decisions."

Trainee Accountant (www.gradjobsuncovered.com)

The life of a Trainee Accountant varies from firm to firm and from division to division. Most will find themselves dividing their time between client work and their studies – both of which will usually involve time away from the office. While all clients have similarities, it is rare to find two that are the same. The location and the people with whom you work can affect the nature of an assignment as much as the subject matter of the business.

"Balancing work and study can be very challenging. It can be very stressful when the professional exams are round the corner and you have to go to work. However, when the exam results are out and I have passed, it is a euphoric feeling."

Trainee Accountant (www.insidecareers.co.uk)

Your work might involve rotations as follows.

Audit involves going to clients' sites and checking their accounting records by performing tests on various balances to ensure that none of the numbers in their financial statements has been 'materially misstated', i.e. by more than the threshold set by auditing standards. Sometimes there are meetings with clients to help understand a specific process in greater depth, but Trainees usually produce working papers and calculations, and then an Assistant Manager will review the work.

"I find auditing public sector bodies really interesting. A lot of what we work on are topics that are in the news and it is interesting to see the point of view of the people working in the sector. It allows you to form your own opinion about what is taking place in the public sector, rather than relying on the media."

Audit Junior (www.insidecareers.co.uk)

Forensic accounting focuses on fraud and litigation. For example, accountants may be involved in investigating fraud and money laundering claims and trying to find out what has happened to the funds in companies. They also get involved in resolving disputes between parties over the value of companies, for example when there is a disagreement over assets during a divorce, or over the purchase price of a company. You may be required to investigate the situation in order to argue factors that show that the value or price should be as low as possible, or alternatively as high as possible – depending on which side of the negotiation you are working for.

> *"In reality, around 90% of the working time is spent out at clients and, therefore, there is a lot more travelling time than I had envisaged."*
>
> Trainee Accountant (www.gradjobsuncovered.com)

Tax work allows specialisation in a particular area early on. For example, corporate tax will help you to learn about the tax calculations for companies and the reliefs that apply. Working in an international firm gives you exposure to the tax regimes and regulations in different countries.

Financial investigations – where a client has a technical problem they don't understand and cannot resolve, such as a balance sheet that will not balance.

> *"This job is not that exciting but the people are fun and the qualification would be worth it even if the job were a lot worse than it is. I would like it without being given time for the ACA, with that I love it."*
>
> Trainee Accountant (www.gradjobsuncovered.com)

Non-financial investigations might include, for example, evaluation of internal controls surrounding a data loss, or assessment of the probity of financial systems and procedures in part of a client organisation. These need a financial background and understanding, but they also need an understanding of how businesses work in terms of people, together with interview techniques, interpersonal skills and a feel for human systems.

Transaction services are based on 'due diligence' procedures on companies' transactions before a merger, acquisition or even listing on a stock exchange.

> *"The job often entails working very long hours in order to get the work complete. Occasionally there is a lack of planning upfront, which results in inefficiencies and longer working hours later on. There is also sometimes a lack of appreciation for the effort put in by junior staff."*
>
> Trainee Accountant (www.gradjobsuncovered.com)

Progression

As you go up through the structure, the fundamental subject matter with which you are working does not change. What changes is your role and responsibility within a project. You will be expected to take on more and more complex tasks, supervise others, plan work ahead, start liaising with clients and gradually working on larger projects.

Eventually, certainly at manager level, you will be assist in pricing and subsequently the day-to-day running of some projects, referring up to a Senior Manager or a Principal (often called a Director, depending on the firm) when you encounter problems, or to have the final work approved and signed off. You will also be expected to help with sales by identifying potential business opportunities and developing client relations, and will have a range of targets to meet, such as the chargeability of your team, the value of direct sales, and the volume and value of 'sell-ons' (additional work sold to a client during a pre-existing project).

Recent job advertisements by the Big Four indicate that candidates for this level should have at least six years' relevant experience, which indicates how long the journey is expected to be from trainee level.

The diagram overleaf shows some of the main pathways available for accountants starting with the Big Four accounting firms. In essence, the experience you gain will be a huge advantage in aiming for any of the destination careers shown, from a Partner at, say, KPMG, through Finance Director at a commercial company, to Chief

Executive of the Audit Commission. It is not unknown for careers to take people out of the major firms only for them to return at a later date after having gained substantial industry experience.

Management consultancy

Management consultancy involves using external hired consultants to do whatever the client organisation needs to do, but cannot do alone because of one or more of the following reasons.

FIGURE 3: Typical career paths for trainees with the Big Four

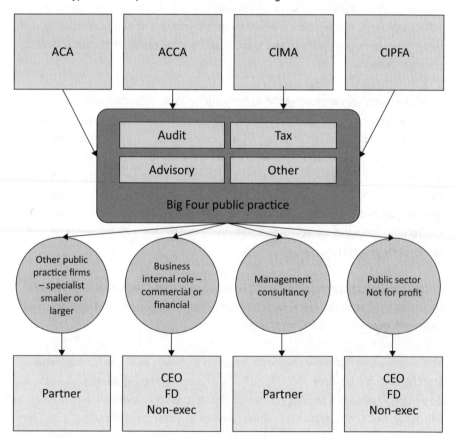

- They lack the capability or the specialist skills required.
- They do not have the capacity to carry out the work within the required timescales.
- They need impartial external advice and assistance to cut through internal politics or to convince shareholders or elected politicians.
- They wish to share the risk involved in the solution.

One of the main reasons for using management consultants is that they have probably already successfully done something similar to what the client wishes to achieve, often many times. From this they develop a 'back catalogue' of best practice, both in terms of practical solutions to issues but also in terms of how best to implement them successfully.

Most organisations, even within an industry or a sector, believe that they are unique and that a solution from elsewhere cannot be 'cut and pasted' across and remain applicable. This is true. However, it is also true that a lot of organisations have many more similarities than they might immediately think. For example, a county police force worked with a commercial national vehicle rescue service to explore how their different techniques for getting a vehicle and an operative (or police officer) to a specific location as quickly as possible might be improved, and both parties benefited.

In the same way, most organisations, while unique, will to a greater or a lesser extent have areas of operational overlap and the same type of support services. In this way many of the building blocks of a potential solution can be found in a consultant's 'back catalogue' and they have the advantage of already having been seen to work successfully.

Despite the increasing pace of change, most senior managers in most large organisations do not, for example, have to run a major change management process more than once or possibly twice in their career. This means that they may have a lot to learn when faced with one, often coupled with a 'day job' to get done and complex internal politics to negotiate. A consultant from a good firm that specialises in change management may have run a similar project six or eight times, will be clearly independent and will have no other priorities than making the project a success.

A brief history

Unlike banking, insurance and accountancy, management consultancy has not been around since the dawn of time. The industry started with the recognition of management itself as a unique field of study and with a company founded by a Massachusetts Institute of Technology professor, Arthur D. Little, in 1886. Originally a technical research organisation, it evolved into the first general management consultancy.

The field grew rapidly during the 20th century as the demand grew for advice, particularly on strategy and organisational design. By 1980, there were only five consulting firms in the world with more than 1,000 consultants. By the 1990s there were more than 30 of this size. Part of this was due to the entry of the major accounting firms into the market in the mid-1980s.

Originally, the 'Big Eight' (now the 'Big Four' described in the section on Accountancy) had always offered some advice alongside their accountancy services. However, as the market for accountancy was maturing, so the market for management consultancy was growing rapidly, at around 20% year on year, for much of the 1980s and part of the 1990s. This was particularly in respect of strategy, the impact of IT and the growing interest of public sector clients.

At this time the market for consultancy was basically two-tiered. There were the big brand consultancies, who charged very large fees, for example over £2,500 a day, plus expenses and VAT, for a consultancy Partner in the early 1990s. There were also a limited number of small to medium-sized consultancies and individual consultants, often ex-Big Four, who worked alone on smaller assignments, teamed up for larger ones, or brought in specialist expertise as needed.

In 2001–2002, the collapse of Enron, the huge American energy company based in Houston, Texas, marked a major change in the management consultancy market. At the core of the scandal surrounding the bankruptcy was the conflict of interest between the advice of the consultants from (then) 'Big Five' professional services company Arthur Andersen and the ostensibly impartial accountancy and audit and services *provided by the same firm*. In 2000, the accountancy firm earned $25 million in audit fees and another $27 million in consulting fees from Enron, so it was not in the interests of some Arthur Andersen Partners to make it clear that their client was not doing anything like as well as it claimed.

Shareholders eventually lost approximately $11 billion, several key Enron executives were tried and subsequently imprisoned, and Arthur Andersen was found guilty of malpractice, 'applying reckless standards' to its audit. It was also found to have shredded several tons of relevant records and supporting documents and nearly 30,000 related emails. The firm's clients deserted it wholesale and the firm rapidly went out of business.

The whole consultancy market contracted, and three of the Big Four accountancy firms soon decided to divorce from their consultancy arms to prevent any suggestion that they could or would operate as Arthur Andersen had done. These arms were downsized and sold off, which released a large number of top-level management consultants into the marketplace, many of whom then set up smaller consulting firms. The increased levels of competition and the nervousness around the use of consultants started to reduce fee levels.

The main 'stagnation' attributable to Enron only lasted from around 2001 to 2003, however, and the market has been recovering since then. Management consultancy, as an industry, reflects the economy and enjoys booms and slumps along with it, but the general trend has been improvement. There was another significant downturn during the global financial crisis of 2007–2009, during which the downsizing of the large consultancy firms to match the contraction of the market again released a large number of top consultants into the market and depressed fee rates yet further. However, the proof of the underlying recovery is exemplified by the fact that all four big accountancy firms have now re-established large consulting arms.

Today, the consultancy market comprises a few large firms, a much larger number of small and medium-sized firms and a still greater number of independent consultants. These can be subdivided into general service consultancies and an increasing number of boutique specialist firms that offer expertise in just one area.

Leading management consultancies

The most prestigious management consultancies in the world probably include:

- **The 'Big Three' global management consultancies:**
  - **McKinsey & Company**: focuses on strategy issues for Fortune 500 companies. McKinsey advises businesses, governments and institutions. It is recognised as one of the most prestigious

consulting firms in the world and has proportionally produced more CEOs in large-scale corporations than any other company. It has 17,000 employees (9,000 consultants). Website: www.mckinsey.com.

- **Bain & Company**: with more than 5,500 consultants, Bain & Company specialises in providing support to private equity firms in respect of leveraged buy-outs and in mergers and acquisitions. It is considered one of the most prestigious consulting firms in the world. Website: www.bain.com.
- **Boston Consulting Group**: specialises in general business strategic consultancy and is recognised as one of the most prestigious consulting firms in the world. It has over 5,600 consultants worldwide. Website: www.bcg.com.
- **The 'Big Four'** – the consulting arms of the professional service companies (described in the Accountancy section):
  - **PwC**
  - **Deloitte**
  - **KPMG**
  - **Ernst & Young.**
- **The spinoffs**: consulting arms of the original ' Big Five' professional service firms:
  - **Accenture**: originally the business and technology consulting division of accounting firm Arthur Andersen, it is now a multinational management consulting, technology services and outsourcing company. It is the largest consulting firm in the world, with more than 244,000 employees. Website: www.accenture.com.
  - **IBM Global Services**: this management and IT consulting firm doubled in size when it acquired the management consultancy and technology divisions of PwC in 2002 in the wake of the Enron case. It is now the world's largest business and technology services provider, employing over 190,000 staff. Website: www.ibm.com.
  - **BearingPoint**: previously the management consultancy division of KPMG but spun off as a separate company in 2000; the organisation changed its name to BearingPoint in 2002 and now employs around 3,200 consultants. Website: www.bearingpoint.com.
  - **Capgemini**: this French firm acquired the management consultancy arm of Ernst & Young Consulting in 2000 and is now a global IT services and outsourcing company with over 115,000 staff. Website: www.capgemini.com.

Management consultancy firms have different specialisms and are largely dependent on the quality and knowledge of their consultants. Here are the main categories.

- **Strategy consulting**: includes developing corporate strategies, business cases, growth strategies; long-range planning; reorganising a company's structure; rationalisation of services and products; and a general business appraisal of the company.
- **Operational consulting, manufacturing consulting or business services**: assistance with process improvement, cost reduction; review of the layout of a production department; production control; productivity and incentive schemes; addressing quality control problems.
- **Marketing consulting**: market research and business forecasting; implementing sales force training; organising retail and wholesale outlets.
- **Financial consulting and management controls**: installing budgetary control systems; profit planning or capital and revenue budgeting; office reorganisation; administrative arrangements.
- **Human resources (HR) consulting**: organisational design; organisational restructuring; talent and rewards strategy; HR policies; staffing planning; job enrichment; job evaluation; employee relations.
- **Technology consulting**: developing technology architecture, technology infrastructure, complex programming; defining information needs; providing software, systems analysis and design; computer feasibility studies; implementing computer applications; computer hardware evaluations.
- **Applications consulting**: advice provided on issues related to large-scale implementation of data software applications such as Oracle, SAP and Siebel.
- **Environmental management consulting**: urban area and regional development planning; international economic research; cost benefit and social analysis studies; physical, economic, ecological and sociological studies.
- **Quality management consulting**: developing strategies; customer satisfaction; performance measurement; people management and processes.
- **Outsourcing consulting**: management of outsourcing projects such as IT, HR or finance.

Different management consultancy firms will cover one, some or all of these specialisms. The re-built consulting arms of the Big Four professional service firms are all general consultancies covering most, if not all, of the above.

In addition to the traditional consulting firms, new models of consultancy are emerging, usually in small to medium-sized companies. Traditionally, consultancies will quote for an assignment or charge on an agreed time and materials basis to produce specified deliverables. Some newer consultancies, for example Practicus, focus on solving client problems and then delivering the necessary solutions in partnership with the clients, their fees being largely derived from achieving the outcomes agreed with the client, for example a percentage of any savings delivered. This means that the extent of their success largely influences the scale of their fees and is known as 'risk sharing' or 'gain share'.

There are also newer forms of consulting organisations, such as Blue Alumni, a firm formed of independent consultants (all with 'Big Four' backgrounds) operating under a single banner to enable them to pool expertise and resources. Another is Red Quadrant, which operates using registered associates rather than permanently employed staff.

Careers in management consulting

Management consultancy is:

> *"Amongst the most interesting, intellectually stimulating and potentially financially rewarding work available in the professional services market"*
>
> *Wikijobs.co.uk*

As a result, it is highly sought after by job seekers and competition for positions at good consulting firms is fierce. Applicants have to show their commitment to a career in this field, academic intelligence and knowledge of the industry (best acquired through work experience or an internship) to have a realistic chance of an offer from the firms you choose to apply to.

Most general consulting firms are organised in a matrix structure. One axis is the business function or type of consulting, such as those listed above. The second axis is an industry focus, such as manufacturing, utilities, public sector or logistics. Together, these form the matrix, with consultants occupying one or more 'cells' in that matrix. For example, one consultant might specialise in operations for the utilities industry, while another may focus on healthcare process improvement. There may be a further overlay relating to the geographic area, depending on the size and scale of the firm.

The opportunities for work experience and graduate schemes we describe below relate to the Big Four firms, PwC, Deloitte, KPMG and Ernst & Young. This is for three reasons.

1. They cover most of the different consulting specialisms.

2. In a business environment where anyone can decide to call themselves a 'management consultant', having big firm experience marks you out as being of a recognised high standard.

3. Their entry qualifications are very high and the competition to work with them is very fierce, so if you are properly prepared to approach a Big Four firm, you are more than ready to approach any other firm.

Graduates starting in consultancy should expect a steep learning curve starting after basic training. The role and responsibilities will vary hugely depending on area specialism and company, but typically graduates do interesting things such as conducting complex analysis, sitting in on interviews, and modelling and preparing client presentation materials.

> *"I enjoy the access to clients, working in a new industry, the strength of some of the colleagues across the consulting organisation. When a job gets mobilised then it is very quickly able to deliver fantastic results to the client."*
>
> *Big Four Graduate Management Consultant*
> *(www.gradjobsuncovered.com)*

Graduates should also be prepared to do the 'less interesting' work, such as preparing documentation, liaising with clients to set up interview programmes, and finding venues for conferences or seminars.

As the work is almost entirely project-driven, a Consultant's working week could be spent in a picturesque European capital or a business park in Slough. A Consultant must be flexible and willing to travel, although the extent to which this is necessary will also vary from firm to firm and speciality to speciality.

Often a Consultant will have to work away from home for several days or weeks at a time, or in some cases for several months. On the other hand, the entirely unpredictable nature of the work means that you may just commute to the office every day for a similar length of time. Increasingly, consultancies are also becoming more open to the concept of remote and home working, so if there is no practical benefit to going to the office, you may be able to work from home occasionally, for example when writing reports.

Similarly, the working hours can vary enormously, but there will certainly be occasions when long hours are needed. This is usually because clients have strict, if not contractual, deadlines by which tasks have to be completed. Very often any delays will be caused by the client themselves (too busy to provide key information, attend meetings, arrange workshops, etc.), but that won't of course make any difference to the project milestones and the required end date.

> "I know I benefited from the time I spent in management consulting. I developed a great problem solving capability and a strong tolerance for ambiguity. In my opinion, those skills alone make consulting a great career investment."
>
> Mark Wong, ex-Consultant (www.randomwok.com)

Figure 4 shows an example of a typical structure in a large management consultancy, but the titles may vary and the smaller the consultancy the fewer levels there are likely to be. As with accountancy, specific projects, client assignments, divisions and departments will all tend to follow this basic design, with different numbers in each layer according to scale.

FIGURE 4: Typical structure in a large management consultancy

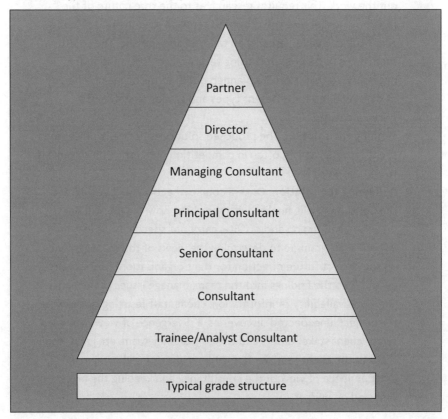

There are fewer graduate entry level opportunities on a pro rata basis in management consultancy than in other areas discussed in this book, as practical experience and credibility in an industry is valued very highly, but there are some.

The work of consultants is project-based and likely to consist of these stages.

- **Finding the lead.** Depending on the sector this can result from a cold visit to a prospective client, or fixed up over a round of golf through an existing client relationship, or a response to an invitation to tender – particularly prevalent in the public sector and for projects over a certain threshold value.
- **Preparing a response.** In order to successfully bid to carry out an assignment, a consultancy must first work out how it would carry

out the work. This requires research as to the true nature of the problem – otherwise the proposed solution runs the risk of being generic and 'vanilla', rather than tailored and specific. The solution then needs to be prepared, using technical or expert input as necessary, so that it can be planned out in terms of the number of days required for different types and grades of staff and a price calculated.

- **Pitching the solution.** The proposed solution is normally presented to client representatives, often in competition with other consultancies, to win the work.
- **Delivering the solution.** Once a course of action has been agreed, the Consultant will: finalise with the client how the job will be organised and run on and off site; carry out specific tasks (e.g. an interview programme to determine the views of top management on the correct future direction for their organisation), write them up and feed the findings into the team; manage issues as they arise (e.g. non-availability of information, client staff resisting or delaying the project, unexpected discoveries, a divergence of views between senior client stakeholders and the consultancy team, etc.) and resolve them to the client's satisfaction while maintaining the impartial independence of view of the consultancy *and* keeping the project on time and on budget.

The role a Consultant plays will vary over time as they acquire experience. In general, they will start on research to support the delivery of the project, and gradually move higher up the list above as appropriate. Every assignment is different, so there is a continual, changing challenge.

One of the complexities of being a Manager in a consultancy is that your assignment team may comprise several Consultants, each of whom may be simultaneously working on one, two or three other assignments for different projects. It can be challenging liaising with other Managers to balance the Consultants' time so that all clients' requirements are met when they need to be, the reputation of the firm is protected and the consultant is not overwhelmed.

The culture of the organisation can make a substantial difference to the experience of working for a consultancy. There tends to be a more collegiate feel in smaller firms, but then if you have a personality issue with anyone it

Birkbeck
UNIVERSITY OF LONDON

Birkbeck is a world-class research and teaching institution

Why study MSc Economics or Finance at Birkbeck?

Our MSc degrees combine a high level of academic rigour with a solid grounding in practical problem-solving skills.

Many of our students work in the finance or economics industry which generates a lively atmosphere with much debate between students and staff.

We have an excellent reputation for the quality of our teaching, providing training for employers such as the Treasury and the Bank of England.

MSc Finance

Students on the Birkbeck MSc obtain excellent specialist training in financial economics including: portfolio theory, corporate finance and advanced pricing theory applied to derivates and government bond markets. Options provide the opportunity to specialise and graduate with a degree in Finance and Commodities or Finance with Accounting.

MSc Economics/Financial Economics

This course is designed to equip a student with tools and techniques for investigating important economic issues and provides a solid grounding in mathematics and econometric techniques. Optional topics include Advanced Econometrics, Industrial or International Economics, Game Theory, Monetary Economics or Forecasting Time-series.

MSc Financial Engineering

This course offers advanced training in quantitative skills used in modern financial institutions, including valuation of securities and measurement and management of portfolio risks. Emphasis is on computational methods and implementation of pricing and risk management techniques.

Open Evenings

Come along to one of our Open Evenings to find out more about the courses we offer and meet our staff. For more information visit:
www.bbk.ac.uk/openeve

---

www.ems.bbk.ac.uk   **020 7631 6429**   **London's evening university**

ICMA Centre

Henley
Business School
UNIVERSITY OF READING

The City offers many financial careers...

...Tailor our degrees to the role you want.

Higher National Diplomas (HNDs)
in subjects* including:

Health and Social Care
Business
Hospitality
Law

Undergraduate 360° programme

Combine a specialist degree, financial career training and
CIMA or CFA® qualification in one programme –
and get a job offer guarantee**.

Other ways to launch your City career

BA (Hons) Accounting & Financial Studies
BA (Hons) Business Administration (Accounting and Finance)
Undergraduate Plus
HND in Business

London
School of Business
& Finance

LSBF.org.uk/city
0203 005 6155
undergraduate@LSBF.org.uk

*Some HNDs are delivered by our partner, St Patrick's.
**T&Cs apply. Some students may not qualify for the job offer guarantee scheme.
The job offer guarantee is solely provided by LSBF, and has no connection with
any other academic partner.

ACHIEVE MORE. BECOME MORE.

can have more of an effect. Similarly, there is a balance to be struck between variety and new experience on the one hand and, on the other, the pressure of having to quickly learn about a new client's company, their industry and the nature of their problems.

Another factor, which is seldom discussed on consultancy websites, is that, certainly in large firms, you are measured on and responsible for your own chargeability – in other words how many chargeable hours you book to clients. To some extent this is 'responsibility without authority' as it is not within your power to control, but you can influence it by 'marketing' yourself internally to ensure that the Managers and Partners setting up jobs know who you are, know what you can do and, therefore, might choose you to be on their team as a job comes up.

> *"I had not expected that we would have to take responsibility for finding our own work. We have to make sure that we are involved in different projects, which sometimes makes you feel like you are self-employed. It is also different in terms of the fact that there is not one person that you have to report to all the time."*
>
> *PwC Graduate Management Consultant*
> *(www.gradjobsuncovered.com)*

Checking websites where consultants write about their experiences – for example www.top-consultant.com, www.targetjobs.co.uk, or www.gradjobsuncovered.com – and networking with people in the industry for their opinions can help you gauge where you might be best suited.

> *"There is no such thing as a relaxing day, and no day is the same. Most of the time this is a positive – and one of the attractive aspects of the job – but at times it can be a downside."*
>
> *Graduate Consultant, Accenture (www.targetjobs.co.uk)*

3

The reality of working in the City

Working in the City can be an overwhelming experience, particularly if you haven't lived there before. Whatever your interests, there will be something for you. There are world-class art galleries, theatres and opera. There is live music of all types, from orchestras to indie bands. There are excellent sports facilities, cinemas, restaurants and night life of all descriptions, as well as beautiful parks. However, a lot of people arriving to work in the City find the sheer number of people on the streets, buses and tube oppressive until they get used to them.

Like all world-class western cities, it is an expensive place to live, which is why many employers pay a London supplement to offset this. Where you live will make a big difference. The closer you are to the centre, the higher the prices for accommodation. The further away, the cheaper. Then again, even in outlying suburbs or towns, the easier a commute into the City, the more expensive accommodation is. In contrast to the cost of your accommodation, the shorter time your journey takes to work, the less expensive it will be. You will have to consider the balance you need to achieve.

Work–life balance

The holy grail of City employment is to find a fantastically well paid, extremely prestigious, extremely interesting job, with loads of time for family and outside pursuits. It is also about as easy to find as the holy grail.

It is common for City firms to say that they take the work–life balance of their staff very seriously. However, to paraphrase the infamous Mandy Rice-Davies in 1963, 'Well they would say that, wouldn't they?' So on the one hand many firms are not up front about the hours you will be expected to work, but on the other hand, if you have done your research (and the people getting internships, graduate entry places or general jobs with these firms definitely *will* have done their research) you should know what to expect.

As a rule of thumb, the more you earn, the more disposable income you will have and the less time to dispose of it. People moving from jobs elsewhere into jobs with the large City firms (e.g. an industry expert coming into management consultancy) are often pleased to find they get large pay rises. They often discover later that although they receive more money, their rate of pay per hour has dropped!

Figure 5 is a rule of thumb guide to what to expect in relation to work–life balance. This is not a scientific analysis, but it correlates with the comments of a large number of new graduate employees on relevant forums and websites. The bottom of the chart represents a 9–5 workplace and the top a 100+ hours a week environment. One of the most complete discussion websites for new graduates is www.thestudentroom.co.uk, which has discussion threads about internships, the application processes and the general experience at different firms, both the big firms and the middle-tier ones. Provided you remember the old rule of marketing, that a person tells four people about a good experience and 10 about a bad one (i.e. people are more likely to be motivated to complain than to praise), it can be quite an informative read.

It is hard to generalise about working hours, but for the middle category in the diagram above, they would probably range from as few as 8a.m.–5.30p.m. to as many as 7a.m.–midnight, but only for occasional projects or specific times of year. Most people will work from around 8a.m. to 6.30p.m. on most days.

FIGURE 5: What to expect in your work–life balance

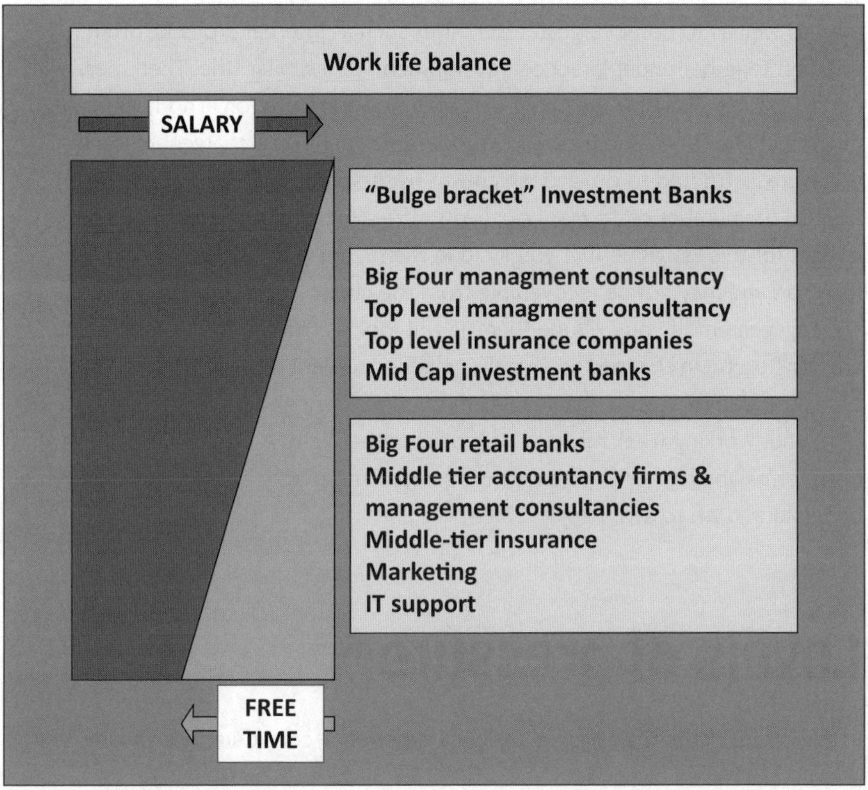

"The main issue is definitely the hours I work. I can be in the office until midnight and it really impacts your social life. There is a general feeling amongst graduates that you have no choice in whether you stay late and will end up having to cancel prior arrangements, which is very frustrating."

City Graduate Trainee 2011 (www.gradjobsuncovered.com)

Most firms operate a time recording system, requiring a day-by-day analysis of your time and what it was spent on in 'decimal hours' (six-minute units of time), to enable coding and billing. You will need to clearly understand the rules and the conventions of how this is to be used. In most firms you will be asked for an accurate list of the actual time spent and the categories of activity each six-minute period was spent on. This would include coding time to chargeable jobs, as well as to non-chargeable activities such as internal projects, often bundled together under 'practice development' or a similar title. Then there will be 'study time' and time we might call 'open to interpretation'. This latter category might include, for example, how you code time spent on a chargeable job that you were instructed to do, and which was necessary, but which was above and beyond the number of days or hours you were allocated in the internal time budget for this assignment. If you include them, they may make your manager look bad and may not be recoverable from the client, depending on the terms of the engagement. If you exclude them, it will look as though you weren't doing anything useful in that period. Another classic problem is travel time. Is travel time recorded? If so, is it chargeable? If not, considering that there might be a lot of it, your working week might start looking rather light. A firm will usually have both formal instructions and extensive custom and practice, and you will need to understand both to avoid any problems.

Levels of pressure

In any career in the City, you are likely to experience considerable pressure.

There will be long hours and an obligation to hit personal and team income and performance targets, in addition to completing your studies. For assignment-based work, there will be periods of work away from home, sometimes with difficult clients. Each different assignment will be a mix of positive and negative factors. For example, in management consultancy a project may come up to develop, say, a single distributed support service between several semi-independent agencies that nominally form part of a central government department – all of which at present have their own support service. With no central authority to instruct the different component organisations to co-operate, you will have to rely on persuasion. This may be difficult, and you may face resistance, as a key objective is to reduce the cost of the service and this means that some agencies will in future receive a lesser service than they have at present. On the other hand, the challenge of designing this service is very interesting, and the senior client managers of the project may be great to work with. However, you may have to live in another part of the country for many months to complete the assignment. Then again, the pay is good and you may get a sizeable bonus if the project is a success.

One of the single biggest determinants of the level of pressure you will feel is how well you get on with your team. If you are working with and for people you respect and like, things are much easier, even if the work and client are difficult. Team members bond together and help each other, which makes the work a lot more manageable. Facing the occasional hostile client under those circumstances is much less stressful than dealing with them on your own.

Another major determinant of the pressure you face will be your ability to say 'no' to people in authority without upsetting them. This is the only way to manage your workload, as no one else will. If you keep saying yes, you will keep being given more to do, which is fine as long as that is what you want, and providing you don't make a serious mistake. If you do, the volume of work you have done will likely be immediately forgotten, while the error will be remembered for a long time.

Working environment and culture

The offices of the firms covered by this book will be of a very high quality, often with an impressive open atrium, a lot of plants, masses of glass partitions and comfortable seating.

Most offices will be open plan, particularly if you are to be a member of fee-earning staff. There is also likely to be a 'hot-desking' regime. This can be as broad as having to find a place anywhere in the building (and you may find yourself working several floors away from your immediate colleagues), or in designated areas identified for different work groups. You will programme the desk phone with your extension so that you can receive your calls and either dock your laptop or sign in to the work station at the desk.

The ratio of desks to staff will determine how easy it is to get a seat in the office and how early you will need to get in if you want to sit in a specific location, but if you are in an open plan office you will also need to get used to a clear desk policy. Simply put, this means you cannot leave anything on the desk at the end of the working day. Most fee-earning staff will be allocated a small area of shelving and any files you need to keep beyond that volume will need to be sent away to deep storage, with agreed retrieval times. You quickly get used to managing this, but it requires self-discipline over what you keep and what you file.

Of course, a lot of work will be done and kept electronically, often on secure shared servers, but it is strange how the long-promised 'paperless office' has never quite arrived, despite the improvements in new technology.

As a fee-earning member of staff, you will be expected to be out of the office a great deal of the time (the actual estimated ratio being the determinant of how many desks there actually are!). This means getting used to living out of an overnight bag and learning to travel light. It is also helpful to travel with some things you might not expect to need but often do, such as a set of travel cutlery, earplugs, an MP3 player for entertainment, perhaps some downloaded e-books on your smartphone. Many executives also travel with a spare good-quality, non-iron shirt or blouse, a spare tie (plain and dark to go with almost any suit and shirt), emergency cufflinks or earrings, a shoe-cleaning kit and a fully equipped wash bag. If you do choose to pack a bottle or a hip flask, as some do – please enjoy it responsibly.

Travel to and from client sites will usually be before or after working hours, so you will need to plan carefully. Many firms have their own travel offices that will arrange flights, trains, hire cars and hotels, etc. for you. However, you also need to know what you are going to do in extremis, for example if you arrive at an airport at midnight and there is no car.

While friendly, most of these organisations will expect their staff to be assertive and confident self-starters. This means that management will normally look for people to come to them with solutions rather than problems. They will expect people to take a proactive role in their own development and in progressing their own career.

The dominant culture is often characterised as 'work hard, play hard'. This means doing whatever hours are required to get your work commitments (over which you will only have limited control) completed to the right quality and the rigid deadline. In general, there is little time in the working day for casual social chat, as people are focused on their tasks and goals. However, working long hours with a group and working at client sites together will often engender a 'Blitz spirit' effect, and teams will bond closely and often choose to socialise together after hours – particularly when away from home.

Mentors

Why you need a mentor

Many organisations will assign you points of contact in the firm when you join. They will often assign someone on the same level as you, perhaps who joined last year, as a 'buddy' to be a first stop for questions about day-to-day issues. They will also usually assign you a supervising manager, even if you don't end up working for that person in assignment-based workplaces, such as at a management consultancy firms. This manager will be the one who carries out your appraisals. Neither of these is the same as having a mentor. One is too junior and the other is primarily concerned with the organisation's interests, not yours. Their primary concern will be the levels of fee income you generate, not necessarily helping you plan your career.

You will also find that the culture in many of these organisations is 'political', to a greater or lesser extent. Just as managing relationships with clients is critical to the business, so too is managing relationships in the hierarchy of the firm you have joined. This can be overwhelming for junior staff or new recruits who do not know how to navigate the culture of the firm, and often the best way to understand all the 'hidden rules' of the business, and maximise your career options, is to have a mentor.

A mentor is another person in your workplace, typically more senior than you (perhaps five to 10 years ahead of you in their career), who is willing to use their own experience to guide you through the organisation and provide advice and guidance for your career. For example, if you are an Analyst or Associate at an investment bank, a mentor could be a VP in another team with whom you have a good friendship, or a Director you play football with at the weekend, or just someone you have persuaded to help you.

Guidelines for picking a mentor

- **Don't choose someone in your own team.** Not only do you need to widen your network, but having a colleague with whom you regularly work as your mentor could potentially lead to conflicts. There is nothing to stop you developing good contacts and people to whom you can go to ask questions, but the relationship with a mentor is rather more significant.
- **Pick someone you respect.** You need someone who can explain the bigger picture for you, someone who is a 'star' in their own field – someone who has really 'made it'. In other words, someone you aspire to be like in a few years.
- **Pick someone you like.** Unfortunately, success and ability do not always translate to an approachable and friendly person. Your mentor is someone you are going to have to spend time with to build a relationship. The more you like them, the easier that is likely to be.

Guidelines for getting a mentor

- **Ask nicely and ask soon.** You are asking someone to give up their limited spare time to help you – for nothing – so keep that in mind. Also remember that it is entirely reasonable for them to say no. Your newly arrived colleagues will also probably be looking around for a suitable mentor, so don't wait too long before asking someone.
- **Be direct and be brief.** Perhaps start with a short email, say two lines. All you need to say is who you are, tell them what you studied and what you do now and that you are interested in their field and would like to learn more. You don't need to ask them to be a mentor straight away – you could just ask to pick their brain and see how that first meeting goes.
- **Be specific.** If you have any common link with them (you went to the same school/university, come from the same home town, follow the same team or are somehow related), say so. Be clear. Be honest. Try to arrange an initial 10-minute meeting over coffee in their office. Most people will be flattered. Some will ignore your email – but that's about the worst that can happen!

Guidelines for maintaining the relationship:

- **Be professional.** That doesn't necessarily mean 'formal', it just means be polite at all times, thank your mentor for help or advice, don't impose on their time, don't gossip, don't criticise others (or the firm!), don't moan and don't ask for favours that could create any sort of conflict for your mentor, such as intervening in a difficult situation not related to them.

- **Make the effort to keep in touch.** Don't stay at your work station and hope for guidance. *Without* appearing to be a stalker, you might seek them out to greet them pleasantly every day, to let them see you have arrived and are ready for work. Try to arrange to get to talk to your mentor every week or so. Regular meetings might not always be possible, but there are plenty of other channels of communication open – so use them.

- **Make the relationship a two-way street.** Try to get to know your mentor and understand their goals, stresses and interests. Share good news with them as well as asking for advice when the news is bad. Follow through on advice or suggestions from your mentor and make sure you tell them how it worked out. If you are going out for food or coffee, ask if they would like some. Get out of the office to meet from time to time, over a meal or coffee; it helps to make the relationship less formal. Always speak well of your mentor whenever you get the opportunity and never break their confidence. If you treat your mentor properly, you could well find that this turns out to be a good relationship for you both that lasts a lifetime, not just the length of your graduate entry scheme.

At the end of the day, what a mentor gets from this will be the satisfaction of seeing their advice bearing fruit and turning young people into successful individuals.

'Up or out' organisations

Most of the organisations described in this book work in fiercely competitive markets, employ top-level graduates and have limited places at the 'top table', which is often a partnership.

This means that, as you go up in the organisation, there are fewer promotion opportunities and more competition. It means that 'standing still' and spending several years in the same role is not usually an option, as there are new graduates coming along behind you. Hence the phrase 'up or out'.

As a result these firms are comprised predominantly of young people at the lower levels, and the average age increases as you go up the structure. In a big firm it is rare to find a member of the fee-earning staff on the first rungs of the ladder who is a senior citizen of, say, 30. Of course, most graduates either can't imagine being 30, or don't believe it will be a problem because *they* will succeed. This may well be so but, for everyone, 30 comes around rather quicker than you might imagine.

The main talent that almost every employer described in this book is looking for (certainly at senior levels) is the ability to bring in clients with lots of money. This process can be applied quite harshly. Bruce F. Webster, an international IT expert and previously a Director at a Big Four management consultancy (http://brucefwebster.com) summed it up as follows:

> "Once a year, each level would do 'stack-rankings' on a fixed curve of all those on the level beneath them. So, for example, the Managers would have to stack-rank all the Associates — if you had 20 Associates, you would have to rate them 1 through 20, with no ties.
>
> Then you would have to apply a fixed curve — say, 10% A, 20% B, 40% C, 20% D, and 10% F. That would mean that of those 20 Associates, only numbers 1 & 2 could be A-rated, 3–6 would be B-rated, and so on, regardless of how much or little separated them.
>
> Those not making the minimum grade (whatever that was) would be invited to leave.
>
> Even those who were above the cut, but who did not score high enough for a certain number of years running, would be informed that there was no promotion to Manager in their future and that they should start looking elsewhere. The

Directors would repeat the same process for the Managers, and the Partners for the Directors."

How these termination decisions are implemented is a reflection of the culture of the firm and of the financial circumstances in which it operates at that point. Overnight sackings of up to, say, 5% or 10% of fee-earning staff have been known in very bad times, but often individuals will be given what amounts to six months' notice that they are going to have to leave and allowed time and resources to assist them to make a good departure. After all, there is often no knowing when ex-employees might resurface as clients in future . . .

Of course, 'up or out' does not tend to apply to internal support services such as IT. However, there tends to be a much more limited technical career structure in IT above Senior Programmer. There may be a few 'architect' positions, and perhaps one post of Chief Technical Officer or similar.

A 'typical' day at work

One of the main things that all the companies we are looking at have in common is being very definite and very firm that there is no typical day at work, as every day is wildly different. To some extent this is true, but it is often true in the sense that your work will follow patterns, and you might find that the pattern changes with each placement into a different department of an organisation, or with each new client assignment you work on.

In general, as a new, junior member of the team, your work will be more closely supervised than it will be later in your career. Your direct exposure to clients is likely to be highest in retail banking as most entry-level jobs and graduate entry schemes involve working in customer service. In the other financial institutions, it is likely to depend on a number of unpredictable factors, such as the nature of the assignments, the attitude of the division you join, the faith in your abilities that you engender in your supervisor, and so on. In general, the more client exposure you get and handle successfully, the more you are likely to receive.

So, with those caveats in place, these are some reasonable and 'possible' days at work for each of the types of firm we are describing.

Retail banking: shadowing a Branch Manager

The day is likely to start at around 8a.m.–8.30a.m., helping with the morning security checks for the branch. This would be followed by a review of the performance or sales figures for the branch, followed by a team meeting for all staff, which may be formal or an informal 'huddle' just to ensure that everyone understands the priorities for the day and to share any new developments.

This would be followed by catching up on incoming emails and company-wide announcements on the bank's intranet.

The morning is then likely to be taken up with meetings, perhaps a team meeting for the management team in the branch, or meetings with community organisations or businesses to promote the bank, often at their premises. Then back to the office to make notes on the meetings and initiating any actions that came from them.

Lunch may not be the full hour when shadowing someone at this level, but there is likely time to eat a sandwich.

The afternoon would probably include several elements, perhaps contributing to an internal training course for branch staff, preparing a report for head office, taking a conference call with other Managers in the region or another meeting with a prospective corporate customer for the bank.

It is also likely to include some unscheduled elements (as most work with the general public tends to do). This could be handling a customer complaint, gathering all the necessary information together from the different services or staff of the bank who have been involved, and resolving it to the customer's satisfaction if possible. One of the reasons this is likely to be unscheduled is that complaints are by their nature not predictable, but also because they then have to be resolved to regulated timescales.

After the doors of the bank close at 5p.m., there is likely to be another short meeting with all staff to get feedback on the day's business and any issues arising; the office cash has to be balanced and the end of day security checks completed.

The day will probably end at about 6p.m.

"Working for a bank is a good job. You get a decent salary, and if you are in sales, your earnings potential is considerable. If you get into a busy branch with a diverse clientele, and you are a good seller, then you can make excellent money. Banks offer competitive benefits as well as discounts on their products and free accounts. Another thing, which to me is one of the most valuable things about working for a bank, is that you will learn about money. You will learn the rules to banking, borrowing money and saving money, three things that you will definitely use in your life. Most banks are very similar – they are nice places to work."

Retail banking trainee (voices.yahoo.com)

Investment banking: Analyst (M&A)

Arrive at the office at 7a.m. and go through the emails for the day ahead. When you are working on international projects, your clients may be in several different time zones. Then set up calls between the buyer and the seller, and their respective lawyers and accountants, in an M&A deal.

Then there may be support work for another project, such as printing and collating pitch books and making sure they get to the relevant Associate in time for their client meeting. Alternatively, there may be an internal meeting or conference call to discuss a new prospective piece of business and whether the firm should take it on.

From late morning to late afternoon (probably no lunch break) you may be involved in 'due diligence' calls, talking your client through the process by which they decided to proceed with this deal to ensure that they have thought of everything reasonable and to identify any outstanding information you believe that they should have – and then putting matters in hand to acquire that information from the other company or third parties such as valuation specialists or lawyers.

Late afternoon to, say, 5p.m. might be spent in a meeting checking what progress has been made between the different sets of lawyers agreeing the terms, conditions and language of the purchase agreement. You may be also preparing a summary of the key points of the Purchase Agreement in plain language to update the client or internal management at the bank.

Between 6p.m. and 8p.m. you might receive amendments from an Associate to a presentation that will be used at a client meeting the next day. Make the necessary changes and pass it back to the Associate for signing off for printing. From 8p.m. to 9.30p.m., print and collate the presentation packs and deliver them to the Associate ready for use.

Finally you could be answering incoming emails and taking telephone calls from a client in another time zone about queries relating to the main deal and clarifying points on the summary of the purchase agreement.

The day will probably end around 10p.m.

Investment banking: Associate (M&A)

The business day would probably start at around 8.30a.m. with a review of incoming emails that have not been addressed on your Blackberry the previous evening, and preparing a 'to do' list for the day. It might be followed by a conference call to discuss a road-show presentation being readied for promotion purposes to a target group of potential clients.

This might be followed by a meeting with a Director and perhaps an Analyst to review the valuation materials prepared for a live merger and identify any supplementary analysis or information needed, allocate the work and agree when it will be finished.

Then there might be an unscheduled meeting with a Managing Director to review the materials prepared for another client project. It is not uncommon for this sort of review meeting with a senior figure to be achieved by waiting patiently outside their office until they get off the phone and diving in to see them before anyone else can. You may wait five minutes or you may wait an hour – but sometimes it is the only way to get enough of their time, when you need it, to complete a project.

Lunch is probably eaten at your desk while answering incoming emails, but there may be time to go outside the building to get something fresh from a local eatery.

For the first hour or so after lunch you might work on the changes and additional material determined for the road-show presentation, and then use comparable recent M&As to value a current live project, in liaison with an Analyst preparing relevant discounted cash flow assumptions to give a fuller picture.

At about 5p.m., you might send the revised valuation materials to the Director for final review before meeting with another Analyst to check on their progress in preparing materials for yet another client.

You would eat dinner at your desk while going through the changes to the valuation materials you just got back from the Director who was reviewing them. After dinner, you would start making those changes and assembling the new information required and arranging for an Analyst to carry out any new analyses necessary.

Once this work is completed and sent back to the Director again, you might finish for the day around 11.30 p.m.

> "Big bucks and long hours are the hallmarks of the investment banking industry. But, if you like fast-paced, deal-oriented work, are at ease with numbers and analysis, have a tolerance for risk, and don't mind putting your personal life on hold for the sake of your job, investment banking may be a great career choice. But if this doesn't sound like you, a job in investment banking could turn out to be a bad dream come true . . ."
>
> Investment banker (www.wetfeet.com)

Accountancy: Audit Trainee

Arrive at the client site at around 8a.m.–8.15a.m. to go through the client's security and entry procedures, showing your ID, signing into the relevant building and sometimes, depending on the client, having your bags searched.

When working on site for a few weeks, there is often a work area assigned to the audit team, but if the audit team is working in a general office, a clear desk policy usually applies, with nothing being left at the client site overnight.

There will be arrangements made for a desk, somewhere to connect up a laptop with access to the internet. There will probably be a photocopier and a printer, but there may well not be a land line available, so remembering your mobile phone charger will be vital.

The first task of the day will be to check incoming emails and see if anything needs urgent attention or changes the plans you had for the day. That done, the morning might be spent interviewing client staff, for example to clarify aspects of the financial records or understand any transactions identified where the company's procedures have not been followed.

How the interviews go will depend on the individuals. Some regard being questioned as insulting to their professional status and resent it. Some may have something to hide. Some may believe they are too busy to devote any time to finding the information you want. Some may be entirely helpful. Sometimes a single day of interviewing can involve all these types of people. Similarly, you may set up a programme of interviews only to have interviewees drop out at short notice or announce as you arrive that they can only give you five minutes.

After the interviews you will need to update your records with the new information you have gathered and perhaps sign off some of the sample transactions you are examining as okay, subject to review by your supervisor.

You may also be asked to give your supervisor an update on progress, and to bring up emerging themes and any issues or obstructions that you would like their advice or assistance on overcoming.

You will probably have an opportunity to stop for lunch. If you are in a town centre, this might mean a few of the audit team go out and eat together or, if you are in an industrial estate in Slough, you might just find an empty office in which to eat your packed lunch.

After lunch you may be asked to prepare a large volume of photocopies of documents needed urgently by your supervisor. Audit Trainees are the most junior people on the team, so they will get most of the basic tasks that come up, such as checking large volumes of figures and even urgent delivery of documents by taxi – Audit Trainees are often a cheaper resource than couriers!

After the copying, you may be examining client documents provided to support the audit or interviewing more staff, depending on what is required. You may also have a session with your supervisor to discuss any coaching points that arise from your work on the project to date.

In the busy season (the first quarter of the year leading to the tax deadline in early April) and on larger audits, you might well work late into the evening or even the night, but the other side of the coin is that across the summer the office hours approach a standard 9–5 pattern. In the busy season, the team might order in a meal to be delivered to the office after the client staff have gone home. There might be a half-hour break for this and then it is back to work. At this time, days ending between 10.30p.m. and 11.30p.m. are not unusual, with whatever weekend working is necessary across the period to get the job done.

The reason for the pressure is that the vast majority of clients will all need their audit done at the same time and all of them have a strict deadline. This is also a busy period for the client companies and organisations, so they may not be able to make their audit their top priority. So, while many delays will not be the fault of the auditors, this doesn't change the date by which the work must be finished.

> *"First day they had me doing VAT returns for some small companies, which was amazing — I thought I'd be on reception or filing. Totally awesome, well, lots of entering invoices (and literally hundreds of receipts!). And the next day I did some bank reconciliation and copying people's bank accounts into our system. I was really worried that I'd be useless having not started the training until September. But they are great and, I think, very understanding."*
>
> *Trainee Accountant (www.thestudentroom.co.uk)*

Management consultancy: Trainee Consultant

The working day can start before you leave your hotel room to head for the client's offices. There may be emails to review and perhaps a phone call from a Manager of the firm to talk about your availability to do additional work for a team on a different project from the one you are on today. This may be work done in addition to your current assignment (often in the hotel after a day at the client's offices) or in parallel, taking up days when you are not scheduled to be on this site.

Most management consultancies are matrix organisations and you sometimes have to be tactful but firm, as six different managers may all want 'only' a day and a half per week of your time, across the same period.

Arrive at the client's offices around 8.30p.m. with your supervisor and start the morning's interviews. The purpose of the interviews may be, for example, to seek the views of senior stakeholders on the future of the organisation, to gather information relating to problems that a client is experiencing, to build consensus and support for a plan of action or to liaise with and manage significant stakeholders for a project – it will depend on the assignment.

As with accountancy, how the interviews go will depend on the individuals: some will find it insulting to be questioned; some will resent it; some have something to hide; some are 'too busy' to spend time finding the information you want; some will bend over backwards to help. Sometimes you can meet all these people in a single day of interviewing. Or you might set up a programme of interviews only to find that interviewees drop out without telling you or can only give you 10 minutes of their time. For whatever reasons, it is rare when a full day of interviewing proceeds as it was originally intended to.

The supervisor will conduct the interviews and the trainee will document them and may be encouraged to ask occasional follow-up questions. The notes taken will probably be handwritten and transcribed afterwards, as it is still seen as rude by many clients to set up a laptop and spend the conversation typing into it.

Lunch will probably be on site and may be eaten at your desk while you check emails and voicemails that have built up during the morning.

In the afternoon, you might be involved in running a workshop for client staff. This might be, for example, to work with them to identify the root causes of specific problems, to hear their views about the strengths and weaknesses of their current operation, to map and redesign selected business processes with which they are involved or to start developing a change plan for implementing a new way of working.

The workshop might conclude at 5p.m. with a presentation by the staff on their ideas and proposals to a senior client manager brought in at the end of the afternoon. Of course, careful guidance and facilitation will have ensured that the proposals are actually practical and sensible. The client manager will only have been committed to hear their ideas and thank the team for their work – not necessarily to promise to use them.

After the workshop, the client may want to discuss how the staff proposals can be used to give additional credibility to the eventual consultancy solution and this may take another hour and a half.

By around 7p.m. you may be back at your hotel, ready to order from room service as you settle down to another couple of hours of reading background materials that the client has provided, extracting useful information as you go and noting any issues that are raised. After a final check of emails at around 9p.m.–9.30p.m. you are 'off the clock'.

> "Management consultancy is never, ever boring. You get well paid, you get interesting problems to solve and you get great people to work with. You may think you are clever before you start consulting, so at first it can be unsettling to come across colleagues far cleverer than you are – but it's the greatest opportunity to learn you'll ever get. The hours and the travel are definitively not family-friendly but, if that's not an issue, then it is a fantastic career . . ."
>
> Management Consultant (practical-consulting.com)

4

Choosing the right path for you

As mentioned in the Introduction, in any of the financial sectors discussed in this book it is very important to know what you want to achieve and what you are aiming for.

The main reason for this is that the UK economy is in one of the worst states it has been in for very many years. This means that a lot of well-qualified people have been made redundant and are looking for jobs. It also means that financial institutions are not hiring in the numbers they used to and are not bidding against each other for the best graduates. It is no longer enough to leave university with a good degree or a good MBA and expect the big financial institutions to throw open their doors in welcome.

In the current job market, having a good degree or an MBA is quite common, and many of the other people who have them may have more experience, better grades or more relevant subjects than you, or have obtained their qualification from a more highly ranked university.

You need to think through whether you plan to apply for a staff vacancy in one of these institutions (direct entry) or whether you will try to join a graduate entry scheme, sometimes called 'fast track'. There are positives and negatives to both. Not all these institutions have direct entry into the fee-earning or professional/ managerial functions. It is entirely possible to join a retail bank as a Cashier and eventually work your way up to Bank Manager. The entry qualifications will be lower than for graduate entry, but the chances of success are probably slimmer and it will probably take a lot longer.

The direct entry route into investment banking involves being a graduate anyway, so for this field the distinction is moot.

You can get into accountancy with a smaller firm by joining as a Clerk or by studying for the Accounting Technician qualification and then (hopefully) persuading your employer to support you in studying to be (for example) a Chartered Accountant. However, this route will again to take longer, although it might be less stressful. On the other hand, you would not have the 'Big Four' brand on your CV, which is a distinct asset if you are looking for a stellar career in the field.

The direct entry route into management consultancy is only possible if you already have a successful track record (probably including a degree) up to senior management in an industry sector in which the consultancy wants to expand.

The larger financial institutions are probably suffering most in the recession and from the poor reputation of 'bankers' that resulted from the global financial crisis. They are still taking on graduates, but the competition is much fiercer. There are still graduate schemes and internships, but there is now less certainty that these will lead to an offer of a permanent job.

All of this means that it is more difficult to get a job, but it is by no means impossible. Here are some of the things you can do, beyond honing your CV and brushing up your interview technique, to increase your chances of landing the job you want. Not everyone knows these things, often because they haven't thought far beyond completing their qualification, but those who *do* know them will have a distinct advantage.

Know which sector you want to work in

It sounds trite, but it affects how you search, what you research, where you apply, who you seek out to network with, and what alternative or supplementary experience you need if you have no job experience at present.

If you don't know what job you want, your chances of getting it are slim.

Know what sort of company you want to work for

The big companies

The big companies are glamorous, well known and still running graduate entry schemes, although they are hiring fewer people because they have suffered most from the reputational damage of the global financial crisis. There are around 50 such firms active in London. They provide more training and bring great credibility to a CV. However, most of their graduate intake have top degrees from the top universities (although some do get in with a lesser degree). In a big firm you are likely to be a smaller cog in that big machine. This will probably mean often working under close direction on something small in scope as part of a larger project. It also tends to mean very long hours. Simon Dixon (author of *Student to CEO: 97 Ways to Influence Your Way to the Top in Banking and Finance*) says that new graduates joining major investment banks should be under no illusions. They will be paid well, but 'You will dedicate your whole life to that investment bank. There will not be any life on the side.' He was speaking of 'bulge bracket' investment banking, which is probably the most extreme case, but the hours required by the top firms in any of the sectors we are exploring will be very substantial.

The medium-sized firms

These are less well known but are faring rather better and also still need new staff. They are not all based in the City. The wages are likely to be lower, there is likely to be less specific training available, but employment with them is likely to be more secure, if less impressive on a CV. It also means a higher probability of getting to see more of the big picture, with more exposure to how things really work.

Small, specialist, boutique firms

These are likely to take on only a small number of graduates each year, but there is a large and growing number of these smaller firms. A few years ago there were very few and now there are over a thousand. They are often set up by groups of 'bulge bracket' or other 'big firm' staff leaving to set up for themselves. They are unlikely to provide training and will expect anyone employed to pull their weight and start contributing value to the firm almost immediately. The firm will usually be focused on a specific market and a specific type of service, but there will often be potential for achievement and rewards not possible in the early years with the bigger firms.

Know what role you want

There are respectable careers to be had in all these sectors, which can be rewarding and quite well paid. However, becoming *really* successful requires excellence and a dedicated pursuit of what you want. You are almost certainly going to have to make a massive investment of yourself, working massive hours under massive pressure. This is why it is important to make sure of the role you want in the sector. If it is something that engages your interest and enthusiasm (or 'passion', as all the recruitment adverts put it), you won't mind the effort, because it will also give you pleasure. But if the role you end up in is not right for you, your working life could become grim.

Movement between work streams (and certainly between employers) within a sector is possible, e.g. in retail banking or in an accountancy firm, but movement between sectors is more problematic, as experience in one sector is not necessarily regarded as useful by another. For example, experience in management consultancy will not facilitate a career in accountancy, and it is very difficult to move from retail banking into investment banking.

"Think about it carefully, and don't jump into the first job you find. There are so many different careers out there and your first graduate job will end up influencing your entire career path, so pick carefully. Think about where you want to live, what sort of hours you want to work, will you be satisfied doing that role and is the salary enough."
Big Four Audit Graduate Trainee (www.gradjobsuncovered.com)

Network with people who do the job you want to do

How many people do you currently know who do the job you want to do? Networking is invaluable. It takes time and effort, but it is worth it. Networking does not mean pestering people for information or help, it means researching and identifying who you want to speak to, and offering them whatever help and information you can, as a means of initiating and developing a two-way, mutually beneficial relationship. Remember, however, that the people you want to link up with will need to see you as credible, helpful and informed if you are to be successful. Then, even if they can't help you directly, they may be willing to introduce you to someone who can.

At the end of the day, if you know the right people, you will get an interview – or may not even need an interview to get the job you want. A significant number of employment offers are based simply on personal recommendations. While your network may not directly result in a job offer, it may help you find out about opportunities, get background information on influential people and companies, and give you up-to-date sector knowledge and access to people with skills and experience that complement to your own.

Adopt the right attitude

There are two parts to the right attitude. The first part is the attitude you display to other people: those you want to network with, those who might employ you and so on. Recruiters report that a large number of applicants come across as arrogant. It's easy to understand why. Most have been told that getting a good qualification marks them out as superior – and they have worked hard and achieved it. Also, they are not applying for careers where the reticent and the nervous tend to succeed. So it is understandable, but it is also not very attractive. 'Positive' – yes. 'Driven' – yes. 'Passionate' (that favourite recruitment buzz word) – yes. 'Arrogant' – not so much.

The second part relates to your approach to putting in the effort and the hours required to get a placement or a job. If asked, almost every candidate would say they are determined and focused on getting their break into a financial institution. But, if we look at this another way, attitude plays a bigger part than people sometimes realise. Most people know that if they eat more calories than they expend in exercise, they are going to put on weight. Most people know that maintaining a healthy weight is good for them and will improve their quality of life and (probably) its duration. Most people also know how to exercise and how to lose weight. So – most people have all the information and understanding required. The next question is, why do most people regard themselves as overweight or not fit enough? There's a difference between the person who knows that going to the gym every day would be good for them, and the person who actually goes to the gym every day.

Decide what your 'brand' is, build it and protect it

As detailed above, you need to narrow down your search and be clear about what you want to achieve. The time of the generalists is drawing to a close and the 'age of the niche specialists' is dawning. How long it will last is anyone's guess, but it will certainly be with us for the short to medium term. In view of this, you need to be clear in your own mind what you are aiming for and why it would be of benefit for anyone to hire you – and remember, the quality of your qualification is not necessarily a distinguishing feature. Once again, if you don't know, you can't effectively communicate it to anyone else.

When you are networking, applying for graduate schemes, requesting an internship or job experience placement, it is now quite likely that the person considering your request will not restrict themselves to reading your CV – they will look you up. This might be through business networking sites such as LinkedIn (which is, incidentally, a good place to search for potential contacts), through social networks such as Facebook or just generally through a search engine such as Google.

What they find will influence their opinion of you. If the first thing they see is drunken photos on Facebook posted by your friends, this may not be a step in the right direction. As far as is realistically possible, everything about you that is publicly available online needs to be consistent and needs to support the way you are trying to portray yourself to a potential employer.

This also connects to the need to try to show your commitment and interest in a particular area through your other activities, work placements, student group memberships and so on. Find out what the recruiters in your specific field value and make sure that they can see that in you. Make sure that any CV you submit is specific to the sector, the firm and the role you are after. This will have more impact than a 'general' CV.

This also means that, if you are applying to a big firm of any kind, applying for internships in every department can create a problem. This is because each division will recruit separately and will want to know from you exactly what it is that makes you interested in their specific area. They will also want to know why you are applying to the other areas if you have said that their opportunity is the one that most interests you.

If you look at the process from the employers' perspective, in the current market they can take their pick from a sea of people with excellent qualifications and backgrounds. Why then should they choose you, if you just want to work for their organisation, over someone equally qualified who has convinced them that they want that *specific* job more than anything else?

In brief, try to take the risk out of the employer's decision to give you a chance.

Prove your value

At its most basic, if you want to get a job, you will need to prove (and probably keep proving) that you add more value to the firm than you cost it. Naturally, this is often relative, both to the value that your colleagues/competitors can prove, and also in relation to how much you cost — hopefully just in terms of your salary and not the consequences of your mistakes.

Be careful what you wish for: you might get it . . .

If you are reading this book with an eye to getting to the *very* top in a financial institution (the six- and seven-figure bonus part of 'the top'), here are a few things for you to think about — over and above how and when to apply and what to expect. This is about groundwork before you reach that point.

First, you need to start *early*. You need to do really well at school and get great grades in relevant subjects, normally including Maths and Economics, plus English.

Then you need to translate those grades into a place at one of the top universities studying a relevant subject, such as Maths or Economics. That said, the actual subject is now less important as you will have proved that you are numerate with your A* grade in A level Maths. What is important, however, is that, if at all possible, your degree should be from one of these universities — in this order (if you study in the UK):

1. Cambridge
2. Oxford
3. London School of Economics
4. St Andrews
5. Warwick
6. UCL
7. Durham
8. Lancaster
9. Bath
10. Exeter.

Source: The Guardian University Guide 2013, **University league table.**

Organisation profile: The ICMA Centre

The ICMA Centre was Europe's first active collaboration between the securities industry and a university finance department when, 20 years ago, the International Capital Markets Association (ICMA) established a new relationship with the University of Reading.

Today, as part of the triple accredited Henley Business School, the Centre offers a range of undergraduate, postgraduate, doctoral and executive education programmes tailored for the capital markets industry.

The ICMA Centre is known for its student-focused ethos, which contributes to both the high achievement rates and the close relationships the Centre is able to maintain with its alumni. This ongoing relationship with its former students provides networking and industry-based opportunities for new graduates and current students. With our alumni based in over 115 countries, these opportunities are global as well as local.

The practical application of finance theory is one of the ICMA Centre's key advantages and is why students and financial institutions alike choose the Centre for their education and training needs. This integration of theory with practice is achieved through the use of the Centre's three state-of-the-art dealing rooms. Equipped by Thomson Reuters with the latest industry simulation software, as well as the Centre's own simulation software platform, ICTrader, the trading rooms have always been an integral part of the teaching and learning style of the Centre. To experience the thrill and pressure of a live market – take positions, quote two-way prices and manage the risk of a $50–100 million trading book – gives our students an insight and experience unavailable in more traditional finance degrees offered elsewhere in the UK.

Our location on the grounds of the University of Reading, only 25 minutes by train to the heart of the City of London, provides our students with the advantage of access to all of the facilities, experiences and amenities open to the students of University of Reading and Henley Business School. The 320-acre Whiteknights campus in Reading provides a wonderful environment conducive to learning.

> *"The degree definitely contributed significantly to my career – if it weren't for the Centre's reputation in the City and the links established with BNP Paribas, I wouldn't be where I am today."*
> *Jake Smith, Fixed Income Derivatives Sales, UK Corporates, BNP Paribas (2010 BSc International Securities, Investment and Banking)*

Organisation profile: courses, internships and career development at the ICMA Centre

Undergraduate degree

The highly focused BSc Finance and Investment Banking undergraduate degree offered at the ICMA Centre is designed to meet the needs of the global finance industry and prepare you for a career in the financial markets. Our practically oriented approach is underpinned by a strong theoretical grounding that equips you with highly transferable knowledge and skills, sought after by leading employers in the sector.

Internships

Students are encouraged to undertake an eight- to 10-week internship during the summer vacation between the second and third years. This invaluable experience will enhance your CV and future graduate employment prospects, help you to build a professional network and provide an outstanding opportunity to apply and further develop your knowledge and skills. Students have recently gained internships at leading graduate employers including Deutsche Bank, Goldman Sachs and Standard Chartered Bank.

Postgraduate

The ICMA Centre offers a wide range of finance-based postgraduate courses from MSc Corporate Finance to MSc Investment Banking and Islamic Finance. There is a growing demand from financial institutions worldwide for specialist professionals trained in the techniques of Islamic Finance. From MSc in Financial Risk Management to MSc International Securities, Investment and Banking, our international body of graduates leave well equipped to pursue a wide range of careers in financial services. Many join investment banks to train as financial markets professionals in trading, sales and research. Some specialise in complex derivative products, while others join brokers and commodity traders. In addition, many graduates follow alternative career paths including consultancy, accountancy, operations, IT, and higher education and doctoral research.

> "I chose the ICMA Centre because of its first-class facilities and professional study surroundings. More importantly, I chose it because of the programmes, content of study and the practical relevance of the course. The dealing rooms, trading classes and projects like the portfolio management challenge are just first class. At the ICMA Centre, one learns the things that really matter to the finance world. They give you the ability to compete and succeed."
>
> Ruven Kloecker (2011 MSc Investment Management)

Career development

At the ICMA Centre we offer the full range of career advisory and professional development services to all our students through our dedicated Career Development Unit. We provide highly focused support, including individual coaching, to give our graduates the edge when applying for career opportunities within the extremely competitive investment banking and securities industries.

Professionals with extensive experience in the City and graduate recruitment staff the Centre's dedicated Career Development Unit. This is an invaluable resource, which can help you to attain your career ambitions. The Unit offers a unique personalised service offering one-to-one coaching and action planning as well as group activities, often led by banking and financial services employees and alumni, on topics such as the preparation of successful CVs and application forms, interview skills, job search techniques and networking.

With a rank of 4th in the UK for careers in 'Accounting and Finance' with the Times *Good University Guide 2012*, and a 96% overall satisfaction ranking with the National Student Survey in 2011, ICMA Centre graduates continue to be well placed to enter the investment banking and securities industries.

Close links with industry

Supported by the securities industry through the International Capital Market Association (ICMA), we maintain close links with the investment banking community. You will enjoy the opportunity to attend guest lectures by senior professionals, including alumni, working within the banking and securities industries. The Centre has accreditation from key organisations, including its CFA Program Partnership and being a CISI Centre of Excellence, and these connections further provide opportunities for our students.

Contact details

ICMA Centre
Henley Business School
University of Reading
Whiteknights
Reading RG6 6BA
Tel: +44 (0) 118 378 8239
Fax: +44 (0) 118 931 4741
Email: admissions@icmacentre.ac.uk
Website: www.icmacentre.ac.uk
Facebook: www.facebook.com/ICMACentre
Twitter: @ICMACentre

Organisation profile

Birkbeck is a world-class research and teaching institution, a vibrant centre of academic excellence and London's only specialist provider of evening higher education. A college of the University of London, Birkbeck ranks among the top 150 universities in the *Times Higher Education* World University Rankings 2011.

You'll be taught by lecturers who are engaged in cutting-edge research and are passionate about their subjects. More than 90% of our academics are research-active and many are renowned world-class experts in their fields. In the most recent UK Research Assessment Exercise (2008), Birkbeck ranked in the top 25% of UK multi-faculty institutions. As a Birkbeck student, you can be sure you're getting an unrivalled teaching and learning experience. The College is recognised for providing the highest quality teaching, and has consistently ranked number one in the National Student Surveys, ranking number one for teaching in 2011.

We are committed to doing everything we can to help students finance their studies and are offering a range of generous financial support packages to complement the student loan scheme. These include reduced course fees and non-repayable cash bursaries.

Birkbeck has all the support services you need as a university student, including a well-equipped library on five floors of the main building on Torrington Square, which is open at evenings and weekends. Library services include a wide range of electronic resources, wi-fi network facilities, access to computers and online book renewal. Networked computer services include high-speed internet connectivity, purpose-built computer classrooms (open 24 hours), facilities for students with special needs and an IT helpdesk with extended opening hours.

The College is situated right at the heart of the University of London in central London (WC1) – and right next door to the University of London Union (ULU) – a well-known music venue. As a Birkbeck student, you have access to all of ULU's excellent sports and social facilities. A central London location means that Birkbeck is particularly well served by public transport – making it easy to get to and from the College.

Case study

Anosh Zahir, aged 31, did an MSc in Financial Engineering at Birkbeck.

Anosh was working as a mortgage broker, but when the recession hit, he decided that the time was right for a career change. Birkbeck's Department of Economics, Mathematics and Statistics has a strong research reputation, and this was a key factor in Anosh's decision to study at Birkbeck. He says: 'I didn't want to learn something from five years ago, or even two or three years ago, as in finance that would be irrelevant by now. At Birkbeck I found that the lecturers knew what was going on in the industry and was really pleased to discover that they were directly involved in the finance sector.'

Anosh found that there was a lot of collaboration between the students on the course. He comments: 'The thing that distinguishes Birkbeck from other universities is that everyone who studies here has made a huge commitment to be here. People either have families, or they're working, so they're here to study hard. That motivation is passed onto everybody else and there was a lot of collaboration between the students.'

This motivation was important, as Anosh explains: 'Financial engineering is a demanding course. You need to be focused. However, the course is structured in such a way that if you are motivated and manage your time, you can get really good grades and come out with excellent knowledge of the subject.'

Having graduated with distinction in 2011, Anosh feels that the objectives he set out to achieve have been accomplished: he has a good degree from a prestigious University of London college and the relevance of the course to the industry meant that he was able to find a good job as a business analyst at a bank in Canary Wharf.

Programmes offered by the Economics Department
All programmes listed are offered on a full or part-time basis by evening study

Postgraduate programmes
PhD in Economics or Finance
MSc Financial Engineering
MSc Finance
MSc Finance and Commodities
MSc Finance and Accounting
MSc Economics
MSc Financial Economics

Conversion programmes
Graduate Diploma in Economics
Graduate Diploma in Finance
Graduate Diploma in Financial Engineering

Undergraduate programmes
BSc Financial Economics
BSc Financial Economics with Accounting

For further information go to: www.ems.bbk.ac.uk

Organisation profile

Westminster Business School, located in the heart of London, is one of the largest centres for business and management education in the UK. The School offers number of specialist business Masters courses, both recognised and accredited by number of professional bodies (namely AMBA, CIPD, CIM, CMI and ACCA) in the areas of:

- Finance and Accountancy
- Economics
- Marketing
- Management
- Human Resource Management
- Business Information Management
- MBA.

The School is also engaged in conducting applied research that is relevant to all areas of business, and much of which has gained an international reputation. Finally, we have built a reputation for enterprise, knowledge transfer in the London region and work with public and private organisations across the UK.

We are London's leading professionally focused and research-engaged business school.

The School is cosmopolitan, having a diverse student population which reflects London's demographic variety and nearly a third of our full-time students come from outside the UK.

Our staff, too, is drawn from many countries, and every year we welcome visiting scholars and researchers from all over the world. Although we are a school with a strongly international outlook, we also draw on a long tradition of providing part-time courses for Londoners. For nearly 80 years the School has served the needs of busy professionals and business people living or working in the capital, giving our full-time students a unique opportunity to network with active business community.

Our strong links with London business and government enable us to bring practitioners and headline-makers into the classroom on a regular basis. In turn we help arrange student placements, internships and mentoring which give our students an important hands-on experience and involvement with the world of work.

The School has growing research and consultancy strengths in a range of areas, including employment research, financial services and international finance, leadership, and business strategy. We host conferences, workshops, seminars and other events open to the public, and regard the dissemination of new ideas to the outside world as an important part of our function.

For more information please visit www.westminster.ac.uk/wbs or contact us at course-enquiries@westminster.ac.uk

Case study

'After working in advertising for five years, I wanted to further expand my knowledge in the field, and after a rigorous search I came to the conclusion that the Masters in Marketing Communications at Westminster Business School was the best choice in terms of academic content, location of campus, and programme relevance. The University was very professional, and responsive to my application.

'Westminster Business School is conveniently located in the centre of London, and you have direct access to most of the city attractions and, most importantly, businesses. The staff are very professional, helpful, and friendly. Moreover, what makes the University of Westminster unique is its rich diversity of international students. Finally, I love the fact that after stepping out of campus after a long academic day, in a matter of seconds you realise that you're back in the busy and buzzing life of London.

'When joining the Business School, you will definitely meet some very interesting people from various different backgrounds and cultures. I was elected Class Representative and that made me push myself more to get to know each and every student in my class. I have built enduring friendships with many colleagues, some of which I will personally cherish forever. It has been very interesting to work on course projects with different people, and see how each approaches academic work differently. I was really amazed by the professionalism and dedication which all students showed. The activities and events that we organise on a weekly basis represent the strong networks that we have built at Westminster in such a short time.'

Fadi Fakih
MA Marketing Communications 2010

'The MBA educated me in management and leadership related issues; it also gave me credentials to facilitate a career move, as it expanded my career possibilities for the future by giving me the big picture and knowledge basis to apply toward a focused career path based on specialised skills. I was actually promoted to a Head of Department while studying for my MBA. Additionally, as an MSc In Information Systems graduate with three years' experience in the field of Information Technology, the MBA Program taught me to see the non-technical side of the business, which was extremely helpful in dealing with non-technical professionals. It provided me with solid business background and analytical skills so that I am more effective in my profession.

'The MBA at Westminster acquainted me with individuals from other fields where the quality of my cohort members was extremely useful to me. Just the interaction with other students was a great value to me, as I learned a lot from their various experience and background.

'Finally, the case studies from all the subjects were relevant, addressing contemporary business issues with a practical focus – from recession to the rising power of China – and delivered by an excellent staff that are passionate about learning and education.'

Nassim A. Ershaed
Head of Bid and Project Management, Pearson
MBA

'A Distinction in my Masters at the University of Westminster gave me the knowledge and confidence to gain a coveted job in an investment bank. Having a solid grounding in theory combined with practice in my Westminster Business School degree enabled me to take on the added responsibilities I needed to advance my career.'

Owen Coughlan, *RBS Global Banking & Markets*
MSc Investment and Risk Finance

On the way, while getting fantastic grades at school and a minimum of a 2.i – preferably a First – at one of the top 10 universities above, you also need to gather the evidence to prove that you are a well-rounded person with a good work–life balance (!). This evidence might include positions of responsibility (e.g. captain or treasurer) in a sports team, or acting in amateur dramatics, playing in a band, volunteering for a charity and so on.

Also on the way, you need to find out how business works. You need to read the *Financial Times* or the *Wall Street Journal* or a similar publication, at least the front page, every day – and you need to do any necessary research to make sure you understand it.

If you are aiming for the top, and particularly the top of an investment bank, you might also consider doing a Master's degree in Business Administration, or an MBA, which typically takes around 20–24 months. Once again, it is important to do the MBA at one of the best schools. In the UK, these are (in this order):

1. London Business School
2. University of Oxford: Saïd Business School
3. University of Cambridge: Judge Business School
4. Warwick Business School
5. Manchester Business School
6. Cranfield School of Management
7. City University: Cass Business School
8. Imperial College Business School
9. Hult International Business School
10. Lancaster University Management School.
    Source: Financial Times Global MBA Rankings 2012

Organisation profile

We are the UK's top provider of finance and business research and education. We also have the ambition and the capability to become Europe's leading university-based business school.

WBS is the largest academic department of the University of Warwick, one of Europe's top universities. Our students come from 151 countries to learn at undergraduate, masters, MBA and PhD level. We nurture top business talent from Britain and abroad through executive education, and develop new knowledge to benefit business and society through our world-leading research.

Masters programmes

Our Masters Portfolio covers a breadth of topics including accounting, marketing, strategy, finance, management and IT. Our Finance suite comprises a range of programmes, including:

- MSc Accounting & Finance
- MSc Finance
- MSc Finance & Economics
- MSc Finance & Information Technology
- MSc Finance with Behavioural Science
- MSc Financial Mathematics.

WBS benefits from excellent links to key financial institutions and employers who support our finance courses. Our courses have benefited from a range of recommendations following consultation with the Bank of England, BlackRock, Citicorp, Goldman Sachs, Merrill Lynch, and many of our alumni. Best practice is embedded in our study programme – as WBS is a CFA Program Partner, employers will know that our finance masters courses equip you with the skills that practitioners need in the field.

Career prospects

The range of companies and organisations in which our graduates work is impressive. It covers many industry leaders, as well as niche players. Some of our graduates also go on to start their own business or work as independent consultants.

Graduates of our MSc in Finance and related courses typically go into roles in investment banking, asset management, corporate finance, and consulting. Warwick is the *second most targeted university* by employers in the UK (according to *The Graduate Market 2011* report by High Fliers Research) and we have strong links with many recruiters.

The university organises annual careers fairs, attended by companies such as Barclays, BlackRock, BNP Paribas, Citicorp, Goldman Sachs, JP Morgan, RBC Capital Markets, and Société Générale. In addition, individual employer presentations are run weekly throughout terms one and two, and sector events run over several weeks, covering sectors including finance and consulting.

All finance students have the opportunity to attend a half-day, sector-specific Career Essentials workshop at the start of their time at WBS. This covers essential topics such as CVs and application forms, looking for jobs, networking, interviews and assessment centres. Additional workshops covering subjects including presentation skills, CVs and cover letters and assessment centres are also provided throughout the year. All finance students have access to as many one-to-one career guidance appointments as they need, as well as individual interview coaching and tailored mock interviews.

For further information please visit www.wbs.ac.uk

If possible, search through your extended network and see if you can find a suitable mentor, perhaps a family member, a university professor or a former employer – perhaps even someone who made it in a financial institution. Make contact with them and seek their advice. They may be a source of wisdom or, even better, the source of an introduction to someone at a big firm.

These steps will all lead towards a very well-paid job, even if it isn't in the institution you originally had in mind. The networking possible at top universities and top MBA schools is an unparalleled opportunity in its own right. Your fellow students are likely to be related to the rich and successful and likely to do very well. They will also probably be able to arrange introductions to the sort of people you need to meet.

But – and this is a very big but – you must be very careful not to confuse money with happiness.

This course of action, whilst maximising your chances of hitting the big time, often comes with a hefty price tag of its own. It is by no means unknown for people at or near the top to suddenly find themselves wealthy, but without a 'significant other' and with few if any friends outside their workplace, because they have no time to find, cultivate and maintain such relationships. They also find they are working enormously long hours at something they do not find fulfilling and which leaves them little, if any, time to enjoy the money they have.

So, as we said that the start of this section, be careful what you wish for. Make sure it is something you really want, because you just might get it . . .

Organisation profile

UNIVERSITY OF EDINBURGH
Business School

The University of Edinburgh Business School enjoys a long tradition of teaching and research. The School offers undergraduate, postgraduate and executive education programmes in business and management and provides a platform for research, discussion and debate on a wide range of business issues.

With a rich heritage of delivering education for over 400 years, the Business School has an international student body typically representing more than 80 countries.

The School has a broad portfolio of educational programmes. These include:

- a substantial suite of undergraduate business programmes
- a suite of specialist MSc programmes, including Master's in Finance and Investment, Accounting and Finance, International Business and Emerging Markets, Management, Marketing, Marketing and Business Analysis, Carbon Finance, Banking and Risk and Human Resource Management
- full-time (one year) and executive (2–3 years) MBA programmes
- a PhD programme and a one-year MSc by research
- a bespoke portfolio of executive education programmes designed exclusively for corporate clients.

The School's teaching and research covers six main subject areas – accounting and finance; entrepreneurship and innovation; management science and business economics; marketing; organisational studies; and strategy and international business. The School is accredited by EQUIS and AMBA and consistently ranked in the *Financial Times* rankings, as well as featuring in the *Economist* rankings for 10 of the last 11 years – reflecting not just a long history of business teaching, but also the substantial experience of a faculty comprising more than 85 teaching staff.

The Business School contributes to contemporary global business and management issues by providing a forum for discussion and debate that brings international academic and practitioner communities together. Many of the School's teaching staff gained significant industry experience before entering academia, and many are active in industry-based research and consultancy for commercial organisations and government bodies. This research work both feeds into the quality of the teaching and provides participating companies with the latest thinking in the field of business and organisational development.

The ethos of the School is to connect degrees, teaching and research into areas felt to be particularly relevant to the business community.

Recently the School relocated to a new building at Buccleuch Place, located at the heart of the University campus. This state-of-the-art space features eight lecture theatres, multiple syndicate rooms, an executive education suite, student study centre and online resource, cafe and significant flexible space for staff and students. The building has been designed and specified to meet the current and anticipated future needs of the School's portfolio of activities and represents an investment of £17m by the University. The refurbished and extended building in George Square provides world-class facilities for the Business School's students.

For more information please visit our website: www.business-school.ed.ac.uk

Case study

Gaelle Nuttall, MSc in Carbon Finance, 2012 student.

I am from France, just near the border with Geneva. As one of the youngest students on the programme I am benefiting enormously from my classmates' experience. We are very lucky with our class, which comprises students of 14 different nationalities with extensive work experience. We have different backgrounds, with some more scientific, others more numeric, so it makes for a very interesting group.

I previously studied business and have had internships working on climate change in Alaska and with a carbon fund in Geneva. I'm very involved in climate change issues and felt the best way of doing socially responsible business was through a Masters in Carbon Finance. I chose Edinburgh because the programme was here but also because of Scotland's 42% emission reduction target for 2020. Scotland's enterprise and the Scottish people's point of view is really important.

The course of study has been great. Our group is spread across diverse backgrounds from carbon markets and financial markets and policy to regulation and climate change issues. The programme gives a great balance of knowledge and an overview of carbon finance that is very grounded in the real world.

The programme involves a lot of personal work. You can do the minimum but you will not succeed. You control your own success; learn as much as you can as this is a great opportunity.

David Kovacs, MSc in Marketing, 2011 graduate.

I previously studied international economics and business and then went on to do an internship in an advertising agency in Budapest and an internship at a digital agency in Milan. I chose Edinburgh because it is a university with a very good reputation.

My classmates were a very varied group and it was great that they had different experiences. Group work exercises were really interesting with so many different perspectives. The School itself is superb, really well outfitted and there are a lot of facilities for work and taking breaks.

I really enjoyed the presentations from external professionals. In particular one of the presentations in marketing application by someone who worked at a digital agency was very insightful. The lecturers on the programme were great and very passionate about their subjects. I would highly recommend this programme.

5

Work experience and internships

Why are work experience placements and internships important?

Work experience and internships are structured programmes in which a student, sometimes at school but normally at university, is invited to join a firm for a period of time, either during the summer break, or for a whole year if they are studying a course that requires a year out in employment – usually called a 'sandwich course'. In general use, the definition of the word 'internship' is starting to blur into 'any paid or unpaid employment for young people'. However, a real internship should contain a programme of exposure to the different parts of the organisation, normally with formal learning of specific skills or knowledge required, and feedback on performance.

From an employer's point of view, the purpose of work experience and internships is to give people the company would probably like to employ in future an opportunity to try working for them before they graduate. In this way they hope to identify the best people, enthuse them and engage their loyalty, so that they will subsequently want to join their firm.

From your perspective, work experience and internships are extremely important in all the financial sectors we are considering because they get your name and face 'on the radar' of the banks, and it is often the case that a successful showing at one event, such as a single day of work experience, may lead to an offer of a summer internship, which can lead to a place on the bank's graduate entry programme. A recent report (*The Graduate Market in 2012*) showed that, of the graduate vacancies at the UK's top employers in 2012, *those employers believed that they would be filling 36% of these places with people who had already worked for them*. In other words, if you are applying and you haven't been on work experience or an internship, over a third of the possible places are already taken. This incremental way into employment with a financial institution is well known, which is why competition for places on work experience is extremely fierce.

In addition to this, most employers either prefer or require work experience on the CV of anyone applying to work with them. It supposedly demonstrates the ability to take on responsibility, a keenness to be employed and, if it is in the right sector, it shows prior experience, which will shorten the learning curve before that person becomes a fully functioning staff member.

Finally, and probably most important, these schemes provide you with the best opportunity to judge whether working for the company in question is to your liking. You get to experience the work, meet some of the staff and get a proper feel for the culture and working conditions. The jobs and careers we deal with in this book will require you to work very hard in a very competitive environment. If at all possible, you need to find out *before* you commit yourself for a period of years whether this is the life you want. If not, you may find yourself working very long hours, under great pressure, doing something that gives you no pleasure; while you may earn a lot of money, you won't enjoy doing it and you won't have much spare time in which to spend it! So if you can make sure in advance that this is for you, so much the better.

This section gives an overview of the opportunities at some of the big firms in each sector. There are also many, many other opportunities with middle-tier and smaller firms, of course, so you should do your research and find the schemes that you think will suit you best. The reason for this focus on the big firms is that these are the 'big ticket' employers, they employ the largest numbers and they pay the most money and so the competition is fiercest. This isn't to say you should work for them. But if you have done your research, and are prepared and ready for the application process at one of the big firms in your field, you are ready to apply anywhere you choose.

Where to find out about opportunities

When internships and work experience programmes are available, they are usually described on a firm's website. There will usually be an online application form and a description of the different stages of the process, which will frequently involve verbal and numerical reasoning tests, plus e-tray or situational judgement exercises – these simulate making decisions under time pressure in an office or client environment. This means that, if you know the sector you want to work in and have researched the main companies in that sector (such as those in Chapter 2) you will be able to keep an eye on their sites to see when applications are invited for their different programmes.

Will you be paid?

The programmes described below relate to some of the most prestigious firms. In general, short events like one- to four-day 'tasters' or two-week work experience programmes are unlikely to be paid, although there will often be an allowance for travel, accommodation and subsistence costs. The longer placements of two months to a year are normally paid, and often include time off to study for professional qualifications (certainly in accountancy).

Many institutions are guarded in revealing how much they will pay people on work experience and internships and, indeed, about how much they pay people in general. Permanent employees are often employed on individual rates of pay, depending on the firm's view of each staff member and how well they may have negotiated their package. This means that two people working together, with the same length of service and doing the same job, may receive very different salaries, as well as bonuses. A few years ago, at many of the most competitive major institutions it was actually a formal disciplinary offence for one employee to discuss their salary with another. This has been relaxed in recent years – which means that such discussions are now merely 'strongly discouraged', but not actually a disciplinary offence.

Saying that competition for these places is fierce is a bit of an understatement, so candidates would be well advised to research in advance what internship they want and why, and be prepared to explain this convincingly to their prospective employer – as well as showing that they meet all the behavioural and attitudinal characteristics required, usually by reference to their extracurricular activities, team activities such as sports and other previous work experience.

Middle-tier and smaller firms also offer work experience and internships, but applicants will (again) need to know how they want their career to develop afterwards to ensure that those internships they apply for will be of assistance. Not all are paid, and not everyone can afford to take an unpaid role. Again, balancing the benefit from the placement against the cost and issues surrounding unpaid work is something for the individual to satisfy themselves about before applying.

What tasks can you expect to be allocated?

You may find yourself having to do some photocopying, making the coffee and other basic support tasks, but that is only because everyone has to. The aim of an internship is not to find cheap temporary labour because, given the length, thoroughness and complexity of the selection process, interns are not exactly low-cost employees. You should expect the employer to make the experience one part real work with the firm and one part familiarisation and training.

The specific tasks will depend on the sector, the particular work experience or internship programme and what aptitude you show while you are there. Normally, you will be assigned work to stretch you and broaden your experience, but there will also be support there to help, because it is not in the interests of your employer for important tasks to go wrong.

To make a success of one of these opportunities, you will have to be 'professional'. There are a lot of definitions of what being professional means, but the one coined by veteran writer and broadcaster Alistair Cooke is probably the most useful to remember:

> *"A professional is someone who can do their best work, even when they don't feel like it."*

Retail banking work experience and internships

As discussed above, work experience and internships can be a very valuable way of finding out if a type of job or a sector is right for you before you commit yourself to a contract of employment that might hold you to your employer for several years.

If, however, you feel strongly that retail banking is the right course for you, the earlier you make contact with the major players, in this case the Big Four high street banks, the better. All of them offer a range of ways of experiencing working with them, including one- and four-day events, 12-week internships (during the summer) and one-year 'industrial placements' (a term for a one-year internship in a sandwich course degree) and it is not unusual for undergraduates to attend sessions with more than one bank.

HSBC's pay and benefits for undergraduates on 12-week internships in 2012 were as follows:

- £350 per week for first-year undergraduate interns and £355 per week penultimate-year undergraduate interns
- up to £4,000 location allowance (depending on where you're based)
- three days' paid holiday
- preferential rates on HSBC products

- discounted travel
- employee recognition schemes.

This reflects the industry standard for retail banking.

All the retail banks follow a similar application process. In general it comprises an online application form, followed by online verbal and numerical reasoning tests. Applicants passing these are then given a telephone interview and those passing the telephone interview are invited to a half- or fullday assessment centre, which will include a final face-to-face interview.

The banks' websites provide information on their specific processes and links to practice tests. Advice on what to expect at each stage and how to best present yourself can be found in Chapter 7.

This section contains an overview and summary of the schemes offered by the four largest independent UK retail banks: HSBC, RBS, Lloyds and Barclays.

HSBC

HSBC run the following work experience and internship programmes.

Discovery Days

Discovery Days, which are held prior to internships, comprise business games and exercises to test potential applicants' abilities. There are practical sessions and presentations providing information on career paths and development programmes within the firm as well as question and answer sessions with HSBC employees and graduates. After the day, those who attend are given constructive feedback about their perceived strengths and tips on areas for development.

Summer internships

Summer internships at HSBC are open to first- and second-year undergraduates on three- and four-year courses of study. There is no restriction on the discipline you are studying, but you must have achieved A grades at both Maths and English at GCSE (or equivalent). Preference is given to people who can demonstrate that they have held some positions of leadership at school or university and some form of customer service experience, either paid or voluntary. You normally need to apply by January for a placement in the summer of the same year.

Full details of HSBC intern schemes and how to apply are on HSBC's Graduates web pages: http://jobs.hsbc.co.uk/graduates.

RBS

In 2011, RBS offered around 600 internships and seem set to increase the number in future. Of these 600 students, over 80% were subsequently offered employment on the graduate programmes, so it is an important step if you are seriously considering a career with RBS. RBS offer the following programmes.

Easter Insight

This is a one-week work experience placement for first-year undergraduates with either the Markets and International Banking (MI&B) or Corporate and Institutional Banking divisions. It offers an introduction to financial services for anyone studying a degree, so you do not need to be studying finance. The placement, which takes place during the Easter break each year, comprises:

- induction
- technical training
- rotation on different desks in the chosen business division
- meetings with senior executives
- networking events.

Over two-thirds of the students attending the Easter Insight in 2011 were offered places on summer internships in 2012.

The closing date for applications is usually the end of January for that year's event, although last year it was extended to February.

Summer internships

These are open to students from any academic background, but you will need to be numerate to succeed. The internships normally last 10 weeks, but some have different durations. They are available in the following divisions:

- Corporate and Institutional Banking
- Business and Commercial Banking
- Global Transaction Services
- Procurement Services
- RBS Finance
- RBS Risk
- Global Restructuring Group
- Security and Risk
- RBS Communications and Marketing
- Corporate Head Office
- Wealth Management.

The first week is an orientation programme, teaching you the basics of banking and meeting the people you will be working with. This is followed by nine weeks of hands-on experience and networking opportunities. You will be assessed twice during the programme and are encouraged to be pro-active in your involvement.

Winter internship programme

This was available last year, but only in the MI&B Banking division, and it lasted for 11 weeks. This programme begins in January and the closing date for applications is expected to be at the end of November of the preceding year.

Full details of RBS internship schemes and how to apply are on the RBS Graduates web pages: www.makeitrbs.com/uk.

Lloyds

Lloyds offer the following work experience placements and internships.

Insight Days

These one-day events take place in several locations throughout the country and are hosted by the bank's graduate recruitment team, plus current and former graduates. Insight Days include:

- an overview of Lloyds Banking Group
- an insight into undergraduate and graduate opportunities
- an assessment centre group exercise and feedback.

Internships (also referred to as 'sponsorship')

Lloyds TSB has 10-week summer internship programmes that are open to people in the penultimate year of their studies who are predicted a minimum 2.i undergraduate degree. The programme runs between June and August each year in the following services:

- corporate markets
- finance
- general management
- business technology
- HR.

In each of these schemes you will have the chance to work on 'live' cases and projects alongside experienced professionals, receiving training in the principles and operation of the bank and the relevant division, and taking advantage of development opportunities. You will meet senior management and have the potential to start developing your own network of contacts. These schemes also give a more detailed indication of what it would be like to be employed by the bank on one of its graduate leadership schemes.

Full details of Lloyds Banking Group introductory and intern schemes and how to apply can be found at www.lloydsbankinggrouptalent.com/.

Barclays

Barclays offer the following work experience placements and internships.

Spring Insight Programme

This is a four-day work experience placement available to 20 undergraduates in their first year of study (or their second year if they are on a four-year degree course). It takes place in April each year at Barclays headquarters in Canary Wharf, London and involves introductions to the following areas of business:

- retail and business banking
- finance
- credit risk
- tax
- technology

- marketing and products
- HR.

The placement will give you the opportunity to shadow current graduates and see the kind of work they do, practise interview, presentation and leadership skills, put questions to senior business leaders, improve commercial acumen through business games, and network. The event concludes with an exercise leading to a presentation to some of the Barclays business leaders, which could lead to a 'fast track' to the final stage of assessment for one of the places on the summer internship programme.

Summer internships

Each year Barclays runs seven internship programmes open to students in the penultimate year of their degree and who are predicted to achieve at least a 2:i qualification. The programmes start in late June and last six weeks. Each internship covers:

- retail and business banking
- finance
- credit risk
- marketing analytics
- technology: product and process development
- marketing and products
- HR.

Full details of Barclays' introductory and intern schemes and how to apply can be found at www.seemore-bemore.com/undergraduate-programmes.

Investment banking work experience and internships

Investment banking is the most competitive and pressured industry in the financial sector, so if you can decide whether it is the right job for you before you commit yourself to a long-term contract of employment, so much the better.

If you have a strong view that investment banking is the right course for you – and you will need this strong view to make it happen – the earlier you make contact with your target banks the better. All of them offer a range of ways of experiencing working with them, including work experience events that last a few days, 12-week internships across the summer and one-year 'industrial placements' (a one-year internship during a sandwich course degree).

Most of the larger banks offer these sorts of programme and, certainly as far as Analysts internships are concerned, a lot of those attending subsequently get offered a place on a graduate entry scheme.

In general the application process for any of the schemes run by the investment banks is similar, comprising an online application form, followed by online verbal and numerical reasoning tests. Applicants passing these are then given a telephone interview and those passing the telephone interview are invited to a half- or full-day assessment centre, which will include a final face-to-face interview.

The banks' websites provide information on their specific processes and links to practice tests. Advice on what to expect at each stage and how to best present yourself can be found in Chapter 7.

As examples we will look at the schemes offered by some of the 'bulge bracket' investment Banks selected as the most popular with undergraduates:

- Goldman Sachs
- JP Morgan
- Citigroup
- Deutsche Bank.

Goldman Sachs

Goldman Sachs is the most popular graduate recruiter in investment banking, evidenced by their winning the Target Jobs Award in 2010, 2011 and 2012. They are also consistently ranked at the top of the investment banking league tables, attract the top talent, and pay the highest bonuses, so no wonder students and bankers all want to get a job at this firm.

It is worth noting that all the Goldman Sachs programmes are open to applicants from across Europe, the Middle East and Africa, so you will face international competition for places.

You will also need to specify the locations and divisions to which you would prefer to be assigned at the time of applying. Be careful about this: while you can edit your personal information once you have submitted your application, you cannot change your preferences. Only select the divisions and locations you are interested in and be clear in your own mind why you have made this choice, because you are likely to be asked about it.

The following schemes are available.

Divisional Spring Internship

This is a two-week work experience placement for first-year students on a degree course (or second-year students on a four-year course of study). The Goldman Sachs website states that they are looking 'for individuals who can balance teamwork and competition, intensity and integrity, intellectual curiosity and leadership potential with a passion for excellence and interest in the financial markets'.

The programme is based in London and covers nine divisions of the bank:

- Finance
- Global Investment Research
- Internal Audit
- Investment Banking
- Investment Management
- Operations
- Securities
- Services
- Technology.

Summer Analyst and Summer Associate

These are 10-week work placements that give you the opportunity to work on live projects of considerable value at Analyst or Associate level. Both programmes start with a one-day orientation course covering the firm and its activities, its culture, and the 'benefits and responsibilities' that go with working for Goldman Sachs. This is followed by training specific to the work of the division where you will be working. After this you become, for all intents and purposes, an employee of the firm doing the real job, working alongside experienced Analysts, Associates and VPs (depending on whether you are on the Analyst or Associate programme). Your work and progress will be continually assessed and successful students may be subsequently invited to join the firm as full-time employees under the New Analyst programme.

Off-cycle internships

These are available ad hoc during the year for students requiring a three- to six-month placement as part of their degree and take place in a number of locations throughout the world. Opportunities are available in the following divisions:

- Finance
- Global Investment Research
- Investment Banking
- Investment Management
- Securities.

Because these are ad hoc placements, there is no specific timetable for applications, which are welcome at any time. Applicants complete an online form and, if Goldman Sachs find it of interest, a recruiter will make direct contact with more information.

Full details of the intern schemes and how to apply can be found at www. goldmansachs.com/careers/choose-your-path/our-programs/emea-programs/emea-summer-analyst.html.

JP Morgan

JP Morgan offers the following work experience and internship programmes.

Schools programme

This is a two-day work experience programme for A level students that runs in July at the JP Morgan offices in Canary Wharf. Successful applicants will participate in:

- classroom-based presentations
- case studies
- interactive seminars
- skills sessions
- trading floor tours.

The aim is to give students a better understanding of what investment banking is and where they might fit in. It also covers public speaking and presentation skills.

Spring Week

The firm runs two different one-week work experience events for undergraduates in March each year:

- Spring Week: Inside the Industry – for those interested in investment banking and IB risk
- Spring Week: Experience the Markets – for those interested in sales, trading and research.

These events are open to any students studying in Europe, from any discipline, in the first year of their degree studies.

Internship programmes

Internships are available in the following areas:

- asset management
- finance
- HR
- IB risk
- investment banking
- operations and business services
- sales, trading and research
- technology
- Treasury and securities services.

Many of the people who join JP Morgan on these internships end up joining them through their graduate entry programme.

Full details of the JP Morgan internship schemes and how to apply are available at http://careers.jpmorgan.com/student/jpmorgan/careers/europe/programs.

Bank of America Merrill Lynch

The bank looks for applicants to demonstrate 'drive, innovation and a genuine interest in the financial markets. Team-working, leadership and problem-solving skills, plus creativity, are key qualities, as is the ability to work in a fast-paced environment, multi-task and interact with a variety of people.'

The firm organises the following programmes.

Banking Uncovered

A one-day work experience programme for A level students. It explains the operation of investment banks and the careers possible in the field. It is held in London and students have a chance to meet and talk with recent graduates about the realities of life at the bank.

Skills for Success

One-day 'introduction to investment banking' events for undergraduates, which are held in spring, summer and autumn. Students can also build up the skills needed for the application and selection process for internships and get hints and tips from recent graduates.

Insight Week

A one-week work experience placement for undergraduates that provides understanding of the bank and progress toward gaining a summer internship. Successful applicants spend a week in London meeting bank staff, taking part in team challenges and developing their application and interview skills. The programme is run in March each year.

Internship programmes

These are intended for students in their penultimate year of study and are available at Analyst and Associate levels. The summer programmes run from

June to August. These are seen as an important stepping stone towards getting a graduate entry position with the firm after graduation. The internships are paid roles, with a one-week induction process and mentoring and a 'buddy' system provided for support and guidance.

Full details of the internship schemes and how to apply can be found at http://careers.bankofamerica.com/campus-EMEA-analyst-associate-internships.aspx.

Morgan Stanley

The bank runs the following programmes.

Institutional Securities: Spring Insight Programme

Run in March or April each year, this is a one-week placement to provide an overview of the Morgan Stanley Institutional Securities Group, which covers: investment banking; global capital markets; sales and trading; research; private wealth management; real estate investing; and investment management. The programme comprises lectures and case studies, plus the opportunity to shadow several desks. Students will also be helped with their communication, presentation and teamwork skills.

Summer Analyst and Associate programmes

These internship programmes are available in the following areas:

- Sales and Trading – Institutional Equity
- Sales and Trading – Fixed Income and Commodities
- Equity Research
- Investment Banking
- Analyst
- Fund Services
- Strats and Modelling
- Strats and Modelling – Quantitative Finance
- Investment Management
- Investment Management – Real Estate Investing
- Private Wealth Management
- Infrastructure – Operations

- Technology
- Finance.

These are all 10–12 week programmes designed to give an introduction to the realities of working in an investment bank, and are designed both to help the student decide whether this is the career and the employer for them and to allow the bank to assess their performance with a view to the possibility of later recruitment to a full-time position.

Off Cycle Internships

These are normally three- to six-month placements and recruitment for them is continuous all year round. The aim of the placements is to enable students to experience the reality of working for the bank in one of the different roles offered.

The Off Cycle internship programmes are:

- Global Capital Markets
- Prime Brokerage
- Investment Banking
- Strats and Modelling – Quantitative Finance Analyst
- Operations
- Technology
- Finance
- HR.

Full details of the Morgan Stanley internship schemes and how to apply can be found at http://www.morganstanley.com/about/careers/index.html.

Insurance work experience and internships

There are a number of insurance firms that regularly offer structured internship programmes. These often run over the summer and will usually be a good introduction to the industry, as well as offering you the opportunity to do some work within one particular area, such as claims or underwriting. The fact that the big firms offer these opportunities, which usually include a competitive salary, illustrates how keen they are to attract good candidates to the business. It also gives those people considering a career in insurance a chance to get a good taste of what the work really involves and, most important, whether this is something you could see yourself doing dayin, dayout for a number of years.

Successfully completing an internship could also put you in a strong position if you intend to apply to one of the graduate recruitment programmes. The following are some examples of the schemes available to undergraduates.

Lloyd's

The summer internship runs from June to August and is open to applicants who are predicted a minimum 2.i degree or equivalent in any subject. The key attributes that Lloyd's are looking for in applicants to the internship are: a willingness to learn and develop new thinking; excellent communication skills and the ability to convey complex information in a clear way; flexibility and the ability to adapt to new situations; and excitement about the business. During your placement you would take on a project from start to finish, and you could be working with Managing Agents to evaluate business plans or investigating trends in claims that are made. There are opportunities to work in most areas and exactly what you do will depend on which area you join. The placement offers you the opportunity to learn about the business and meet key people. Should you complete the internship successfully there is also the possibility of being offered a guaranteed place on the graduate scheme.

For more detailed information about internship opportunities at Lloyd's, see www. lloyds.com/lloyds/careers/graduates/internship-programme.

RSA Group

The internship programme runs over eight weeks during the summer, usually starting in early July. Placements are available in three disciplines (actuarial, underwriting and claims) and could be either in London or at one of their regional offices.

In order to apply you need to be on track to get a minimum 2.i degree in any subject, unless you want an actuarial placement, in which case you will need to be studying a relevant actuarial or mathematics-related degree. If you successfully complete the internship there is also the possibility to get direct access to the graduate programme.

For more information about the internship programmes at RSA Group, see www.rsagroup.com/rsagroup/en/careers/graduate_programme/ ukinternshipprogramme.

AIG

The summer internship programme runs over 12–14 weeks and is open to applicants who are predicted a minimum 2.i degree (or equivalent) and have already achieved a minimum of 300 UCAS tariff points (or equivalent). The scheme is also open to graduates who have a minimum of a 2.i degree. Candidates also need to have strong written and oral communication skills and must be able to demonstrate an interest in pursuing a career in the insurance industry.

Successful applicants work closely with mentors and are assigned objectives so that their progress can be monitored on a weekly basis. Although interns are assigned to a particular business area, there is also the opportunity to gain exposure to other business areas to broaden your knowledge of the business.

For more information about internship opportunities at AIG, see www.aig.co.uk/ intern-programme_2538_389243.html.

Accountancy work experience and internships

The main thing that distinguishes a career in accountancy is the pressure of the first few years, when you have to excel at learning the day job (usually audit) while passing a series of complex, difficult exams in order to qualify as an accountant. With most accounting firms you will have done this on a graduate entry scheme and a training contract that commits you to a working for the company after you have passed the exams, so that the firm can recoup its investment.

This means that it is a very good idea to get as much experience as possible of what it is like to work for one of these firms before signing up for the next five years of your life. For many people, it is an interesting and fulfilling career with plenty of variety. If you find, for whatever reason, that it is not for you, it is better to do that before you are contractually tied.

We will look at the schemes offered by the Big Four accountancy firms below. Many other firms also offer internships and you can normally find details on the firm's website.

PwC

Summer internships lasting six weeks are available for students in the penultimate year of their studies. Succeeding on the internship could mean an immediate offer of a place on the graduate entry scheme after graduation. The internships are in the following business areas:

- assurance
- tax
- actuarial
- financial advisory.

In addition to summer internships, there are also business placements in all PwC services, which are open to students on four-year sandwich degree courses. There is no specific application method, so it seems that a direct approach to the firm for more information would be the best place to start.

Full details of the PwC intern schemes and how to apply are available at http:// www.pwc.co.uk/careers/student.

Deloitte

The following programmes are available at Deloitte.

Summer vacation scheme

The Deloitte Summer Intern Schemes are seven-week paid programmes. Each placement includes an induction and the necessary technical training to enable applicants to work alongside experienced staff on live internal and client assignments.

The main summer intern placements available for accounting each year are:

- professional services rotation – including two of audit, tax and risk consulting – ERS
- actuarial.

Industrial placements

The Industrial Placement programme is designed for students who are required to undertake a business placement as part of a four-year degree course. It gives them the opportunity to work in different Deloitte offices across the UK and in a range of different service lines:

- audit
- tax
- consulting – technology
- corporate finance – analytic and forensic technology and enterprise risk services.

The placement starts alongside Deloitte's annual graduate intake and, after initial training, students carry out the role of a first-year graduate working in one of the above areas. The recruitment process and academic criteria mirrors that of the firm's graduate roles.

Full details of the Deloitte intern schemes and how to apply are available at http://mycareer.deloitte.com/uk/en.

Ernst & Young

With all programmes, applicants can be studying any degree. The firm looks for applicants with evidence of positions of responsibility and any recent work experience, as well as other skills, such as team working, communication and analytical ability.

The following schemes are on offer.

Insight Days

These one-day visits to an Ernst & Young office are open to undergraduate students. They will show you how the business works and you will take part in a team case study of a client problem.

Leadership Academy programmes

These are three-day residential events open to undergraduates. The structure feels like half assessment centre and half leadership skills workshop. The programme runs three times a year and there are up to 24 places per session.

Summer internships

These are six-week placements open to penultimate-year undergraduate students. There are a total of 250 places on the three summer placement schemes, which are run in London and two other regional offices across the summer. The programme dates are normally staggered, with the first starting in June and the last finishing in September each year. Specific dates for each event are on the company's website.

After induction, students will start working full time alongside graduates who have just joined the firm, working on live projects and assignments with clients in one of the following:

- advisory
- assurance
- corporate finance
- tax.

Supervision, mentoring and periodic feedback are provided to help interns develop in the role. Successful interns may be offered a place on the graduate entry scheme for the following year, returning to the same team they have been working with.

Industrial placements

These 10-month placements are available to penultimate-year degree students who are looking for a placement working with a professional services accountancy firm.

Successful applicants could be working on live projects and assignments, shadowing one of the firm's Partners, and studying for and sitting some of the professional accountancy exams.

Placements are available in the following areas:

- advisory
- assurance
- corporate finance
- tax.

Full details of the Ernst & Young work experience schemes for undergraduates and how to apply are available at http://www.ey.com/UK/en/Careers/Students/Your-role-here/Students---Undergraduates#fragment-0-na.

KPMG

KPMG offer a number of different programmes. In addition to the standard application criteria, KPMG looks for specific characteristics in successful applicants, notably that they:

- deliver quality
- drive collaboration and inclusion
- strive for continual improvement
- exercise professional judgement
- make an impact
- are aware of and seize business opportunities
- demonstrate innovation and curiosity
- display resilience.

Gap Year Programme

This is a six- or nine-month work experience placement aimed at students taking a year off between A levels and university and who are thinking about a career and qualification in accountancy. KPMG provides supervision, mentoring and development opportunities. Areas of experience covered include working for different clients, shadowing one of the Partners of the firm, as well as networking and social events. There are programmes in these areas.

- **Audit**: a six-month placement from October to March each year, working with a team in the Audit practice.
- **Public Sector Audit**: a six-month placement from October to April each year. This team provides services to key areas of the UK's public sector, such as health, central government, local government, housing, education, and other publicly funded non-profit organisations.
- **Risk Consulting**: a nine-month placement with a team assisting its clients to manage their regulatory environment, extract value from their financial and organisational risk management processes, and develop high-quality governance and corporate sustainability.
- **Transaction Services**: a nine-month placement from October to July each year. The team advises clients through the deal cycle, from pre-deal planning to post-deal support. They assist clients to buy, sell and finance businesses.

Easter internships programme

This is a two-week placement in March or April each year, in either Tax or Audit, available to students in the first year of their degree course.

All programmes start with a one-day induction programme. Interns will then work alongside full-time staff and clients on live projects and assignments both at the KPMG offices and at clients' sites. Supervision, mentoring and regular feedback on progress are provided to help interns develop in the role.

Vacation programme

These are only available to students in the penultimate year of their degree studies. They run for four, six or eight weeks, depending on the business area, and normally start in June or July.

Summer vacation accountancy internships are available in the following areas:

- audit
- public sector audit
- tax
- pensions
- risk consulting
- transactions and restructuring.

One-Year Business Placement programme

This is aimed at students in their penultimate year of a degree course with a sandwich placement and offers internships in either the Audit or Risk Consulting Technology arena. In addition to working on live projects and assignments, both internally and with clients, successful applicants for the Audit internship will have the opportunity to take time off to attend college and study for the first stage of their professional qualification, the ACA or the ACCA.

Full details of the KPMG internships and how to apply are available at http://www.kpmgcareers.co.uk/VacationProgramme/default.aspx?pg=1954.

Management consultancy work experience and internships

As a sector, management consultancy is expected to employ around 2,000 people on graduate entry schemes in 2012 (Association of Graduate Recruiters (AGR) *Graduate Recruitment Survey 2012*). The hours may be less punishing than in investment banking, but they are still not family friendly, and neither is the amount of time you are likely to spend living away from home while working at client sites. While you would not be signing up for the five years of the standard accountancy training contract, leaving a job shortly after you join generally looks bad on a CV, but staying in a high-pressure job you are not enjoying might necessitate that. So, as with the other sectors we have reviewed, it is important to know if this field is going to be the correct one for you before committing yourself to it.

The examples listed below are the schemes offered by the Big Four Accountancy firms. Many other firms (such as the leading firms detailed in Chapter 2) also offer internships, and details can usually be found on the firm's website. In each firm, the short-term events such as 'taster days' and three-day experience workshops are common to both their accountancy and consulting recruitment processes and the full details of the application processes are covered above.

Summer internship and business placement programmes are simply shorter versions of the graduate entry programmes, which are described in detail in the next chapter.

PwC

PwC offers summer internships, one-year business placements and graduate entry programmes in consulting. The minimum educational requirements for all these are 340 UCAS points from the applicant's top three qualifications, not including re-sits, and a predicted or achieved 2.i degree in a subject depending on the specialism.

Full details of the PwC intern schemes and how to apply are available at www.pwc.co.uk/careers/student.

Deloitte

Deloitte offers summer internships, one-year business placements and graduate entry programmes in consulting. The minimum educational requirements for all these are:

- an A or B in Maths and A–C in English Language GCSE, obtained in the first sitting
- 320 UCAS points from the applicant's top three qualifications, not including re-sits
- a predicted or achieved minimum of a 2.i degree, in a subject depending on the specialism.

Full details of the Deloitte work experience and internship schemes, and how to apply, are available at http://mycareer.deloitte.com/uk/en.

Ernst & Young

Ernst & Young offers summer internships, one-year business placements and graduate entry programmes in consulting, which they refer to as 'Advisory'. The minimum educational requirements for all these are:

- minimum B grade in GCSE Mathematics and English Language
- at least 320 UCAS points at A level (not counting General Studies or re-sits)
- a predicted or obtained 2.i degree.

Full details of the Ernst & Young work experience schemes for undergraduates and how to apply are available at www.ey.com/UK/en/Careers/Students/Your-role-here/Students—-Undergraduates#fragment-0-na.

KPMG

KPMG offers summer internships, one-year business placements and graduate entry programmes in consulting. The minimum educational requirements for all these are:

- minimum B in Maths and English Language GCSE from the first sitting
- 320 UCAS points from the applicant's top three A levels, not including re-sits or General Studies
- a predicted or achieved minimum 2.i degree, in a subject depending on the specialism.

Full details of the KPMG work experience and internship schemes, and how to apply, are available at www.kpmgcareers.co.uk/VacationProgramme/default.aspx?pg=1954.

6

Graduate recruitment programmes

Direct entry or graduate entry scheme?

Just to recap a few important points from Chapter 4: there are alternatives to graduate entry schemes for some of these employers, usually referred to as direct entry, where an applicant gets a 'normal' job with a financial institution and works their way up. There are advantages and disadvantages to both routes. In some institutions direct entry into the fee-earning or professional/managerial functions may not be possible. You could join a retail bank as a cashier and work your way up (starting with lower qualifications), but you will need to be a graduate to secure a role in investment banking, whether you choose direct entry or a graduate scheme.

In insurance, there are some opportunities for direct entry, but most entrants go into the industry via a graduate scheme. The benefits of a graduate scheme are that you should get structured and formal training in your chosen field and perhaps be given support to study for some of the professional qualifications available to people working in this sector. Once you have experience and some industry-specific qualifications, progress can be quite quick and you could be working as a Loss Adjuster within four years. Similarly, in accountancy, direct entry is available at a lower level, but the route to the top is likely to be longer than if you join as a graduate.

Direct entry into management consultancy is rare unless you already have a successful track record (probably including a degree) up to senior management in an industry sector in which the consultancy is interested to expand.

The larger financial institutions are probably suffering most in the recession and from the poor reputation of 'bankers' resulting from the global financial crisis. They are still taking on graduates, but the competition is much fiercer. There are graduate schemes and internships, but there is now less certainty that these will lead to an offer of a permanent job.

Finding the opportunity

All the big firms have some form of graduate entry scheme, whether it is a limited time contract, a training contract or a fast-track programme for their professional or executive staff. These are advertised on their websites, which usually contain full details of entry qualifications, the application process and the deadlines involved. If you are an undergraduate, the other main route for approaching financial institutions is through their 'milk round' presentations at university campuses, where they will be trying to attract top-quality candidates who have not so far been involved in their work experience or internship programmes. It is worth checking with the organisers of employer presentations at your campus to find out which organisations will be attending and when, as well as keeping an eye on the websites of firms that are of particular interest to you.

Because of the levels of competition and the fact that it is currently a 'buyers' market', the financial institutions do not attend every university. If you are at one of the top 10 universities in the UK, you can certainly expect a visit, but if you are in one of the much lower ranked ones, it is highly unlikely. It is also worth finding out about such visits in advance because they are often constructed like assessment centres, rather than lectures, which means the number of places may be limited and allocated in advance.

Another advantage of checking is that, if your university is not on the circuit for, say, the investment bank of your choice, that bank may respect your initiative if you contact them directly to check whether they are happy for you attend a session at a different university in the area. They may not allow this, but it is always worth asking. If you don't ask, the answer is a definite 'no'; but if you do ask, the answer may still be a 'no' but it also *might* be a 'yes', so what have you to lose?

The application process for the graduate entry scheme of almost every financial institution is the same as those detailed for internships in the previous chapter, unless you are offered a place as a result of a successful showing on an internship programme. It comprises an online application form, followed by numerical and verbal reasoning tests, a telephone interview, an assessment centre and, often, another face-to-face interview. Details of what to expect at each stage and how to show yourself at your best in the application process can be found in Chapter 7.

Is a graduate entry scheme right for you?

The important thing to understand is that getting a place on one of these programmes is not the end of the story. These programmes are a great opportunity, but they are also another form of test – not a guarantee that you will start your career with the firm in question. If you do really well, it is highly likely that you will be welcomed in with the offer of a permanent job, or at least another fixed-term contract with the firm. If you do not do well, you will be out when the scheme finishes.

In this section, we will look at the graduate schemes offered by some of the big firms for their fee-earning or revenue-generating professional or executive staff. We will focus on them for the same reasons that we looked at their work experience and internship programmes, i.e. these are the 'big ticket' employers: they employ the largest numbers, they pay the most money, and so the competition is fiercest. As mentioned before, this isn't to say you *should* work for one of these firms, and there are many, many other opportunities with middle-tier and smaller firms. The point is that, if you have done your research and are prepared for the application process at one of the big firms in your field, you are ready to apply anywhere you choose.

The pros and cons of each scheme vary. On the one hand, there is the credibility of a major name on your CV. You are also likely to be earning more than most new joiners to any of these firms, which is good, but it might also mean that if you don't perform or don't pass your exams, the firm may decide to cut its losses and let you go early. Then again, if the firm has made an investment in you, they may decide to give you as much support and help as possible in order to get their return.

You will almost certainly be contracted to stay for a given length of time, usually two or three years – which means that either you could be let go at the end of that period or you may have to stay even if you don't particularly want to. A contract tends to be longer (normally three to five years) if you are studying professional qualifications, so that the employer can get some return on their training investment. It is highly unlikely that there will be leeway for negotiating changes to the terms and conditions of a graduate or MBA entry scheme, so study the small print and make sure you are happy to be bound by it.

The bottom line is that there is no right answer. There is only the right answer for you. You will need to get all the information and weigh your decision.

Retail banking

The banks in this section account for almost all the UK's retail banking graduate entry schemes, reflecting the dominant position held by the Big Four high street banks. These schemes are also the main route through which the banks recruit the staff who go on to become their senior managers.

All of them have graduate entry schemes, the details of which are described below. They also have MBA entry schemes, but these are on a different and much smaller scale; one bank, for example, only takes 25 MBA entrants per annum. In general, the structure and application process for these is very similar to that for graduate entry, and details can be found on the banks' websites, which are given at the end of each section.

The fundamental components of each programme at each bank are broadly similar.

- **Orientation and introduction**: covering the basics of banking, finance and branch operations. In addition, entrants will be set overall programme goals, so that the practical experience they gain contributes to a strategic overview of the role of bank management.
- **Placement 1**: learning the branch basics. It's all very well being a Manager, but if you don't have first-hand experience and understanding of the actual jobs that your staff perform, the management task itself becomes a lot harder. No matter how good your degree or which university you went to, banks will insist that all senior staff spend some time in the branch network. You will be tasked with everything from basic cashier work to assisting the Manager. You will also be expected to continue learning and completing the projects set as part of the overall graduate programme.
- **Placement 2**: further experience in other functions. This basically involves learning about related services such as credit card operations or small business banking, as well as spending time in regional offices learning the operational functions. In terms of understanding the bigger picture, you will also study the business challenges facing banks.
- **Professional qualifications**: at this level, most banks will offer you the chance to take professional qualifications, and expect you to pass them as a part of your career progression.

Once you have successfully completed your training, you may be offered a permanent position at the bank, potentially becoming a Senior Branch Manager, looking after either a large branch or a group of small branches – this is how most people start. Alternatively, you could move into regional management, supporting Regional Managers. You could move into a central role and get specialist experience in areas such as marketing, project management, IT, operations or compliance. Some graduates are taken directly into these roles, but retail bankers also have the opportunity to move into these functions at a later date.

HSBC

Retail banks in general are thought to be good places to work, and HSBC has a better reputation that most. It won the award for Graduate Employer of Choice 2010 and for Most Popular Graduate Recruiter – Banking, Insurance and Financial services in the Target Jobs, National Graduate Recruitment Awards 2011 and 2012. On the other hand, the *Independent* newspaper reported in April 2012 that HSBC would be cutting around 2,000 jobs, predominantly management positions on its retail banking side, so the impacts of the global financial crisis are still being felt.

The bank offers two-year graduate development programmes, with the possibility of a permanent position with the bank on successful completion of the scheme. There is no guarantee of a job at the end of the scheme and an offer of employment will always be based on a number of factors, including the current state of the economy and the performance of the bank, how well the applicant fits the culture of the firm, whether the primary skills of the applicant are currently in demand and so on. In other words it is a business decision.

The graduate programmes cover the following areas:

- commercial management
- executive management
- retail management
- customer propositions
- technology and services (HTS) management.

Full details of HSBC's graduate schemes can be found at http://jobs.hsbc.co.uk/graduates/graduate-programmes/.

RBS

The bank runs a wide range of graduate schemes in different business areas, including several in different support functions of the bank. The website does not discuss salaries beyond calling them 'competitive', which probably means that they are in the order of £25,000–£35,000 a year. It is possible that the support function graduate programmes may pay slightly less.

Given the range of schemes available, RBS recommends that applicants think long and hard about which they wish to apply for and why. The application process will also ask why the graduate is applying to RBS, what attracted them to it and why they think they would be a good investment for the bank.

Full details of the RBS graduate programmes can be found at https://continentaleurope.rbsbankyoubuild.com/graduates.

Lloyds Banking Group

The graduate programmes offered by the bank are in:

- corporate markets
- finance
- general management
- business technology
- HR.

Full details of the Lloyds Banking Group graduate programmes can be found at www.lloydsbankinggrouptalent.com/programmes/?graduates-programme-large.

Barclays

All programmes begin with an induction week, and include formal training events and provide sponsorship and support to study for professional qualifications, as well as on-the-job development. There is periodic individual feedback on progress and a 360-degree evaluation process.

As at 2012, the salary for graduates on the scheme was a base salary of £36,000, with a joining bonus of £8,000, the potential for a performance-related bonus, payment in lieu of pension, private healthcare and other benefits. Part of the programme is likely to be based at the Barclays Global HQ in Canary Wharf, but other elements could take place across the UK or internationally.

Full details of the Barclays Future Leaders two-year graduate programmes can be found at www.seemore-bemore.com.

Investment banking

While your putative employer might see work experience as 'desirable' rather than 'essential', and will more routinely expect you to have done an internship, a very good degree from a very good university is an absolute necessity. The only way for new entrants into investment banking is via a graduate entry scheme, which all major banks run. If you don't have such a degree, the only alternative is (allegedly) to be related to a very senior investment banker. As in so many walks of life, who you know can often trump what you know.

With almost all the larger investment banks offering graduate entry schemes, there are a lot of places to aim for, but you need to be aware of the level of competition and the reason *why* there are so many places on graduate schemes each year.

First, competition: around 80% of employers insist on a minimum of a 2.i degree, so a 2.ii degree, which used to be entirely respectable, is now (at least for these purposes) of very limited value. This is as a result of 'grade drift' over the last decade or so. In the 1970s (when far fewer people went to university) only around 2% of students achieved a First; now that figure is around 15%–20% and (according to timehigherseducation.co.uk) a total of 64% of students in 2011 got either a First or a 2.i degree, nearly two-thirds more than was the case even 10 years ago.

The result of this is that the number of graduates chasing places on internships and graduate entry schemes has also grown. In July 2012, it was reported by the BBC that there were at least 80 applicants for every graduate post within the financial sector where competition is toughest.

The final reason why investment banks have a continual requirement for new graduate Analysts is that almost all of them are routinely 'let go' at the end of their three-year graduate entry contract. A few do make the jump up to Associate from a position inside the bank where they have been working. More decide to study for advanced qualifications before trying to join an entry scheme for Associates.

This chapter contains an overview of the graduate schemes for Analysts and Associates run by the bulge bracket banks.

Goldman Sachs

As mentioned earlier, Goldman Sachs is the most popular graduate recruiter in investment banking, as shown by their success in winning the Target Jobs Award in 2010, 2011 and 2012, but this may be because it has a reputation as the most prestigious bank that pays the highest salaries, rather than because it is a good employer. It is also consistently ranked at the top of the investment banking league tables, attracts the top talent, and pays the highest bonuses, and this is why almost all the best students and bankers want to get a job at this firm.

The Goldman Sachs graduate recruitment programmes are as follows.

- **New Analyst Programme.** Applications for this programme are accepted from final-year undergraduate- and graduate-level students from any field of study, with no specific requirements for work experience. While the subject of the degree is not important, an outstanding record of academic achievement and a strong, detailed interest in the financial markets certainly is. This is a three-year programme and the firm is looking for people who are specifically interested in Goldman Sachs rather than just interested in investment banking.
- **New Associate Programme.** Applications for this programme are accepted from final-year students working for an advanced degree such as an MBA, JD, MD or LLM. Successful candidates usually have two to five years of work experience. Again, the subject of the degree is not important, but a level of knowledge of the industry and the products and services Goldman Sachs offers is expected.

Full details of the graduate schemes and how to apply can be found at www.goldmansachs.com/careers/students-and-graduates/our-programs/emea-programs/index.html.

JP Morgan

JP Morgan stresses the importance of applicants researching and understanding as much as they can about the investment banking business in general, about JP Morgan and about their preferred areas of the business *before* starting an application.

Each successful graduate accepted onto a two- or three-year programme will have an individually designed programme that is adapted to his or her needs and determined by the Manager. As part of the training, all graduates receive an introduction to the company, the products it offers and how the team they are joining fits into the business as a whole.

Full-time graduate opportunities are offered in each of the following areas of the bank:

- Asset Management
- Audit
- Finance
- Investment Banking Risk
- Investment Banking
- Operations and Business Services
- Private Bank
- Sales, Trading and Research
- Technology.

Full details of the JP Morgan graduate schemes and how to apply can be found at http://careers.jpmorgan.com/student/jpmorgan/careers/europe/graduate.

Bank of America Merrill Lynch

The bank offers graduate programmes in these main areas:

- Chief Financial Officer
- Global Consumer and Small Business Banking
- Global Banking and Markets
- Global Risk
- Global Wealth Investment and Management.

It looks for applicants who demonstrate 'drive, innovation and a genuine interest in the financial markets. Team-working, leadership and problem-solving skills, plus creativity are key qualities, as is the ability to work in a fast-paced environment, multi-task and interact with a variety of people.'

Full details of the graduate schemes and how to apply are available at http://campus.bankofamerica.com.

Morgan Stanley

There is a very wide range of graduate Analyst programmes with the bank, not all of which are available in the UK. The full list can be found at http://www.morganstanley.com/about/careers/programs/associate.html.

There are programmes available for the UK and Europe in the four main divisions of the bank:

- Institutional Securities
- Investment Management
- Infrastructure
- Company Management.

Full details of the Morgan Stanley graduate schemes and how to apply are available at www.morganstanley.com/about/careers/index.html.

Insurance

Most of the big employers in this sector offer graduate schemes, so it is worth doing your research and looking at their websites to see what is available. Below is a selection of some of the schemes available to give you a taste of what is out there.

Lloyd's

There are two graduate programmes on offer at Lloyd's. The Generalist Graduate Programme is for those who want to become business leaders. It is an 18-month scheme that offers you the opportunity to choose three placements from a range of options, which means that you can tailor your training to your areas of interest. As well as learning on the job you will also have some more formal training through workshops, seminars and lectures. The scheme is open to anyone with a minimum 2.i degree (or expected 2.i) in any subject.

The Claims Graduate Programme is for those who know they want to specialise in insurance claims. During the 12-month scheme you would have two placements, the first in a broking house and managing agency and the second in a law firm. There are opportunities for jobshadowing, giving you the opportunity to see all aspects of work in claims. In addition there is also some formal training through workshops and seminars. As with the general programme you need to have (or be expecting) a minimum 2.i degree in any subject in order to apply.

For more detailed information about internship opportunities at Lloyd's, see www.lloyds.com/lloyds/careers/graduates.

RSA Group

Graduate schemes are available in actuarial, claims or underwriting. Each programme lasts two years and offers structured training and development. You will be offered plenty of support, as well as leave for study and a mentor to help you through your placement.

For more information about the internship programmes at RSA Group, see www. rsagroup.com/rsagroup/en/careers/UK_internship.

Chartis

Chartis runs an actuarial programme and an underwriting programme for graduates. Both are structured training programmes over two years that offer you the opportunity to experience the full breadth of the roles with a view to developing a long-term career.

For more information about internship opportunities at Chartis, see www. chartisinsurance.com/intern-programme_2538_389243.html.

Accountancy

In relation to the availability of graduate entry schemes, there was, according to the AGR *Graduate Recruitment Survey 2012*, an overall 20% reduction in the number of opportunities available in 2011.

Accountancy, however, remains the largest employer of graduate trainees in the UK, with around 3,500 places predicted for 2012 (an increase of 1.5% over the previous year) and a correspondingly large programme of work experience and internship programmes.

The graduate schemes, which include support for studying for exams, are all some form of training contract, whereby the trainee is obliged to stay in the employ of the firm for (usually) two years after they qualify, and if they fail their exams at any stage they run the risk of being dismissed.

Since the banking crisis, there has reportedly been a shift towards accountancy trainees opting to study with middle-tier firms rather than the Big Four. In surveys more younger accountants are reporting that they believe they will get greater exposure to client work with the middle-tier firms and that they now have a greater distrust of the largest firms – both FTSE 100 clients and the Big Four firms themselves.

This may be true, but clients still respect the value of the Big Four brand on a CV and these firms are still the biggest and most prestigious accounting firms around, with the largest numbers of opportunities for graduate trainees.

PwC

PwC runs graduate entry schemes in each of the five main divisions of the firm:

- Actuarial
- Assurance
- Financial Advisory
- Tax
- Technology.

Full details of the schemes and how to apply can be found at www.pwc.co.uk/careers/student.

Deloitte

The firm offers graduate entry schemes in five major divisions of the business:

- Audit
- Corporate Finance
- Drivers Jonas Deloitte (Real Estate Advisory).
- Risk Consulting
- Tax

Full details of the Deloitte graduate entry schemes and how to apply are available at http://mycareer.deloitte.com/uk/en/student/apply-now/academic-requirements.

KPMG

KPMG graduate programmes normally start in the autumn of each year, but the firm recruits to these programmes on a rolling basis and all applicants are dealt with on a first come first served basis. However, some business areas and some offices do fill quickly, so it's advisable to apply sooner rather than later.

Graduate programmes are concentrated into three main areas of the business: audit, tax and pensions. There are programme places based at all the different offices around the UK.

Full details of the KPMG graduate entry schemes and how to apply are available at www.kpmgcareers.co.uk/graduates/.

Ernst & Young

There are programmes starting in September each year in three main areas: assurance, tax and corporate finance.

Full details of the Ernst & Young graduate entry programmes and how to apply are available at www.ey.com/UK/en/Careers/Students/Your-role-here/.

Management consultancy

PwC

PwC offers graduate entry programmes in management consulting and can also offer deferred places for graduate entry in some cases: if, for example, an applicant wants to take a gap year for a specific project. The applications and qualification process is identical, and the place is taken up one year later.

Consultancy is organised into several streams, each of which has a graduate entry scheme:

- management consulting
- economics consulting
- risk consulting
- strategy consulting
- sustainability and climate change consulting.

Full details of the PwC graduate entry programmes and how to apply are available at www.pwc.co.uk/careers/student.

Deloitte

The Management Consultancy Graduate Entry Scheme is a 21-month programme covering the development of consultancy skills. In the first four weeks every graduate completes a professional qualification. Analysts in People and Programmes, Customer, Finance, Strategy and Operations will complete Foundation level CIMA (Chartered Institute of Management Accounting) training. Those in Technology Integration will study a two-week Information Systems Examination Board (ISEB) course.

After this initial induction all new consultants will have a two-week residential training course in consulting skills, based in Scotland. This includes a realistic 'Introduction to consulting' case study, taking graduates through a full consulting project lifecycle. The case study is realistic in that trainees will be expected to work in a team to produce high-quality deliverables. On return from Scotland there are competency inductions ranging from two days to one week, at the end of which graduates will move onto actual work teams and start their first client engagements.

The training and development at Deloitte continues throughout the programme. In addition to on- the-job training there are both instructor-led and online learning courses.

There are graduate entry schemes in the following streams in consultancy:

- actuarial
- customer
- finance
- technology
- operations
- strategy
- people and programmes.

Full details of the Deloitte graduate entry schemes and how to apply can be found at http://mycareer.deloitte.com/uk/en/student/university.

KPMG

KPMG describes management consultancy as one of the fastest growing areas of their business. They run three graduate entry programmes for management consultancy:

- Management Consulting
- Management Consulting IT Advisory
- Management Consulting Business Technology.

Full details of the KPMG graduate entry schemes and how to apply are available at www2.kpmgcareers.co.uk/graduates/graduate-programmes/.

Ernst & Young

The graduate entry schemes in advisory services (Ernst & Young's term for management consultancy) are in these areas of the business:

- Actuarial
- Financial Services Advisory Consultant Programme
- Advisory Consultant Programme
- Advisory Consultant Programme – Technology
- Information Technology Risk and Assurance (ITRA)
- Financial Services Risk.

Full details of the Ernst & Young graduate programme in management consultancy and how to apply can be found at www.ey.com/UK/en/Careers/Students/Graduate-Opportunities.

7

Getting your first permanent role

Looking for a job

If you are looking for an internship or a graduate entry programme, the best place to start is the websites of the specific institutions that you are interested in, having identified those through your background reading and research.

If you are looking for a 'normal' job in banking, there are specialist web pages for banking vacancies, such as www.bankingvacancies.com. In addition, there are more than 20 specialist recruitment agencies for banking and investment graduates in London with whom you can speak and perhaps register your details if they do not have an immediate vacancy. The UK Recruitment Agency Directory (www.agencycentral.co.uk) keeps an up-to-date list of these agencies, together with their websites, telephone numbers and other contact details.

Agency Central also lists 60 recruitment agencies specialising in accountancy and finance positions. In addition to this, the Institute of Chartered Accountants in England and Wales (ICAEW) maintains a website – www.icaewjobs.com – which has details of hundreds of vacancies for Chartered Accountants.

There are also specialist recruitment agencies for management consultants. These can usually be found advertising individual vacancies on the recruitment pages of www.top-consultant.com. Amongst the most active are:

- Mindbench: www.mindbench.com
- Selecture: www.selectureglobal.com
- Consulting Point: www.consultingpoint.co.uk
- Beament Leslie Thomas (BLT): www. blt.co.uk.

You will also find a large number of advertisements placed directly by management consultancies.

What are employers looking for?

It's simple, really. Employers are looking to appoint someone who will turn out to be exactly the person they were looking for.

Unfortunately for employers, people are unique individuals with different strengths and weaknesses. Therefore, in order to maximise the chances of finding what they are looking for, employers will try to minimise the risks of making mistakes.

The selection process

Traditional application form

If you are applying for a direct entry position, rather than going for an internship or a graduate entry position, there is a strong possibility that you will be completing an application form online, but in a more traditional format. This means it will come up as an analogue of a paper form, allowing you to look at the questions and fill in your answers in blank text boxes.

The key to making yourself stand out in this type of application is to take your time. You will often find that you can work out your answers in another programme, such as MS Word, and then cut and paste them into the form once you are satisfied with them. This means you can make sure your spelling is correct too!

Lay out your information as neatly as you can: line up any lists or tables, such as employment history, and explain any gaps or overlaps. Make sure the information you provide is self-contained and self-explanatory.

There is usually a free text section for you to explain why you are a good match for what the firm is looking for. Make sure you write this specifically for this application and for this firm. Anything generic is quickly spotted by a recruiter and looks both lazy and as if your application to that firm isn't that important to you. Become very familiar with any job description and person specification provided and re-read the advertisement (if you are responding to one). Then tailor what you say to play back to the employer what they have said they are asking for. Don't do this by repeating their words back to them, but by selecting experience to write about and paraphrasing their adjectives.

For example, if the advertisement asks for someone 'passionate about customer service excellence', a suitable response might be to reference some work (or life) experience of dealing with customers (or the general public), and saying how much you enjoyed it because you have always found that successfully sorting out problems for people always gives you great personal satisfaction.

Online forms and tests

With internships and graduate entry schemes where a large applicant response is expected, many employers will try to save time and ensure that the people they take all the way through the interview process are reasonable 'bets' by using online application forms. These forms are often used to screen out obviously unsuitable candidates, for example on the grounds of academic attainment. To take a popular set of requirements, if someone does not have, say, 320 UCAS points from their top three A levels, not including re-sits or General Studies, they will often find that they cannot progress to the next question on the form, but are rejected immediately.

The remaining applicants will then usually find themselves tested with online verbal and numerical reasoning and other psychometric tests. The verbal and numeric reasoning tests usually have right or wrong answers, while psychometrics are there to test judgement and personality.

As with IQ tests, it is generally believed that practice improves scores, and there are many sample tests available on the internet, for example:

- www.psychometric-success.com
- www.kent.ac.uk/careers/psychotests.htm
- www.careerpsychologycentre.com
- www.shldirect.com

Please note that no claim is made that these are representative of any specific industry, or that these are the best sites available for practice tests. Many of the major employers either have practice tests on their websites or put up links to those sites they believe will be most helpful to applicants.

Telephone interview

The first stage of the selection process may be a telephone interview. You should treat this as a proper job interview and prepare in the same way as you would for a face-to-face meeting. The interviewer is looking for you to demonstrate to them how well you align with the competencies their firm is looking for. This is done by reference to things you have done and achieved, particularly in your extracurricular activities such as voluntary work, sports or hobbies. Most firms list the competencies they are looking for on their website, so read these and become familiar with them, and think about what examples you are going to use to demonstrate, for example, that you are a team player, that you have leadership potential, that you can take on responsibility, that you can use your own initiative, etc.

Remember that the other important thing you need to impress upon them is how much you know about the role you are after and why you want it. This can often be done by thinking of good questions to ask the interviewer. At this stage, never ask questions like how much money they will pay you. There will be plenty of time to agree that later.

Write out some mock questions and practise answering them aloud. Recording yourself and listening back to what you said can be instructive: you will be able to hear whether you sound nervous, pompous, too talkative or, alternatively, both confident and competent – which is what you are aiming for! Another way that recording yourself helps you is by showing you how fast you are speaking. It is very common for people to speak much faster when they get nervous or excited. Unfortunately, inside your head, you will think you are speaking at normal speed, but the person you are talking to might think you are gabbling. Recording yourself will help you hear whether you are doing this. If you are, the answer is to try to deliberately speak slowly, which has the double benefit of both helping you think ahead to structure your answer better, and also bringing you back down to what others will hear as normal talking speed. However, *you do need to listen to a recording of yourself before you do this* – something that a lot of people shy away from because they don't like their own voice. If you don't, and then speak deliberately slowly when you don't need to, you will still sound strange, just in a different way!

The interviewer will normally telephone you, so be ready, sitting down at a desk or table, five or 10 minutes before the agreed time. Take the call somewhere quiet where you can compose yourself and then concentrate. Be friendly but focused. The interviewer is not out to trip you up; in fact they will probably try to give you the best chance to shine – but they won't hesitate to write you off if you don't.

Have a pen and paper ready to make notes. Have a list of key points you want to get across and a list of questions you want to ask. Have a copy of what you submitted (if possible) or a copy of your CV. Have a glass of water, just in case. Put your watch on the table before you start, so you can see how much time has passed and how much is left. It is fair to assume that the interview will last 30–45 minutes.

Remember that the start and end of an interview leave the greatest impression, so be confident, friendly and positive when saying hello and when signing off, perhaps with something like 'Thanks for speaking to me today, and I look forward to hearing from you in due course.'

Always remember that there are lots of other firms if this one doesn't prove to be a good fit, so don't build it up in your mind into something frightening. If they didn't think you were worth speaking to, they wouldn't call you . . .

Assessment centres

Employers are often looking for a complex mix of collaborative, assertive people who are also highly competitive and determined to succeed, but who do not (hopefully) alienate those around them in the process; hence assessment centres.

These usually last between a half day and a whole day. The actual tests involved and their sequence will be determined by the firm and the industry it operates in, but most assessment centres have a similar basic construction, so what appears below is a 'worked example'.

1. **Numerical tests.** These will be similar to the one you passed at the earlier stage of your application and to those you can find online, but they will almost certainly be harder, often progressively as you go through the test. Try to work quickly, especially on the easier questions, to leave you more time at the end. The marking scheme for tests differs: some only consider completed questions; but most take into account how many questions have been attempted. It is very common for these tests to be designed to be too long to complete in the time allowed – so do not be downcast if that happens.

2. **E-Tray exercise.** This requires you to deal with a set of incoming emails as if this were a day on the real job. It is basically an update of a very old selection exercise called the 'in-tray exercise'. There is usually a time limit on these tests so, if possible, it is best to skim read all the emails and take very brief notes before starting to try to answer or resolve any of them. This is because some of them will be irrelevant; some will imply that a certain type of response is required, which may turn out to be the wrong way to go because of incoming information three emails later and so on. Again examples are available online, for example here: faststream.civilservice.gov.uk/How-do-I-apply/Example-e-Tray-Excercise/.

3. **Group exercise.** The subject matter varies, but whatever the subject, you will be assessed on how you work in groups. This group is often a small one of between four and six people. You may, for example, be asked to read some material and then discuss it and come up with a potential solution or review the conclusions it reaches. The observers will be looking for you to show leadership, to see your influence on

others, how you engage with other people and how they listen to you. Show original thinking and interpret the information: don't take it for granted – propose different solutions from the ones that you have read, and so on. Demonstrate that you can think outside the box. Put a lot of energy into that exercise. Make your presence felt, but don't be aggressive. You will also need to watch your time, as it is likely that no one will tell you how much time you have left.

4. **Interview.** This will be very like the telephone interview, but more personal. The most important thing is to keep as calm as you can. If you can think yourself into enjoying the process and liking the interviewer, that's half the battle won. As this is face to face, your body language and clothes will also be under scrutiny. If you are not advised of a dress code, use the one for the firm's offices, which you may have seen in person, or can gather from their website. Remember, it's not always possible to guess right, but it is always better to be slightly too formal than too informal. Once again, the start and finish of the interview are the points that will make the greatest impression. Among other things, you will be assessed on your ability to get 'on a wavelength' with the interviewer or interviewers. One strategy is to try to get someone (preferably someone who works as a Manager) to give you some mock interviews before you go to the assessment centre.

5. **Presentation exercise.** You will be given a sheaf of papers and asked to read them and then make a presentation of your proposals for resolving a fictional situation. Read carefully, make notes and organise the information. Some of it will probably be irrelevant. Be sure of your solution and leave yourself plenty of time to write it up (probably on a laptop or flip chart). When presenting, *do not read your slides to the audience*. This is an amateur mistake. If you have ever had to sit through a presentation in which someone simply reads out their slides you will know that it very quickly becomes extremely annoying. Assume that your audience are literate and capable of reading for themselves. If in doubt, ask them if they can see clearly, or if they would like you to read any of it. What you say should expand on what's written, comment on it or clarify it. Make your case clearly, dynamically and confidently and show commercial awareness. Be prepared to answer strong (if not hostile!) questioning afterwards.

You are looking to present yourself as an outgoing, friendly and confident person. You need to be seen to take part and to be comfortable working alongside the others present, contributing when you have something pertinent to add and listening closely to what others contribute. Employers are not normally looking for dramatics, attention seekers, people who speak first and think second, people who are sarcastic and aggressive or people who withdraw and stay silent.

Every now and then you may not understand what has been said. Then you will have to decide if it is important enough to ask for clarification – if it is, ask. Do not be afraid of making yourself look bad in front of the other applicants. If you didn't understand, the chances are that several of them probably didn't either. Remember that in business communication, it is the responsibility of the speaker to be clear, not for their audience to understand.

Most important, you must try to present the most positive aspects of who you really are. You may successfully act your way through an assessment centre, but remember that working at this firm is likely to be similar in tone to the assessment centre itself. If you pretend to be something you are not, this may be difficult or stressful to maintain in an everyday work situation – and perhaps this isn't the job for you after all.

Key skills

So what sort of skills are employers looking for? We list below some of the skill sets that employers are likely to be testing for in their application process for a sample of the entry-level jobs in each type of financial institution. Unsurprisingly, for entry-level positions in related financial industries, there is considerable overlap. For example, it is inevitable that any position is likely to require familiarity with PowerPoint, but these are included in each category, so that each is complete and self-contained.

Retail banking

Trainee Bank Manager

The key skills of a Trainee Bank Manager (either direct entry or graduate employment entry) include:

t's a jungle out there

ery one of our finance courses has been
esigned with top-level input from leading
ancial institutions, ensuring our graduates
ave us with the skills to succeed and thrive
the competitive world of finance.

MSc Finance
Ranked the UK's number one pure finance
course by the *Financial Times*, and in the
world top ten.

::: **MSc Finance & Information Technology**
Learn to use your quantitative skills
in the City and on Wall Street.

::: **MSc Finance with Behavioural Science**
Explore human decision making and its
impact on the financial world.

::: **MSc Business (Finance & Accounting)**
For ambitious non-business graduates
seeking a career in finance.

wbs.ac.uk/go/cityguide

THE UNIVERSITY OF
WARWICK

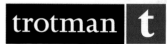

- excellent skills with Excel spreadsheets, MS Word, PowerPoint
- work prioritisation and planning – balancing conflicting deadlines and changing timetables
- a high level of financial numeracy and an ability to use statistics
- ability to assess financial and business risk on a day-to-day basis
- good communication skills, both written (concise, thorough reports) and oral (excellent in meetings and persuasive presentation skills)
- handling client telephone calls confidently and reliably
- ability to build an effective and productive internal network with the relevant key people
- ensuring the accuracy and quality of the work of any staff assigned to work for you on projects or on a permanent basis
- ability to lead and motivate and manage staff to meet targets
- good marketing, sales and IT skills
- a business-focused attitude, with a good knowledge of the local economy
- ability to deal courteously with customers (some difficult), with tact and confidentiality
- ability to communicate effectively and build long-term working relationships with existing and potential clients
- ability to negotiate, solve problems and make effective decisions
- high levels of integrity and honesty
- ability to work productively and harmoniously as part of a team
- ability to adapt to change
- language skills (if working in investment or international banking).

According to trainees, the keys to success include:

- getting the assigned tasks done to time, to quality and to budget without complaint
- taking on as much as you possibly can, without the risk of failures – which means being able to (very occasionally) say no when asked to take something on
- asking for help when you need it and being helpful to others when you can
- getting on well with colleagues and bosses
- networking effectively – but don't gossip
- having a positive mental attitude and an outgoing personality

- leading others by example
- dressing neatly.

Investment banking

Analyst

The key skills of an analyst include:

- excellent skills with Excel spreadsheets, MS Word, PowerPoint
- excellent skills with a Bloomberg Professional services terminal
- excellent research skills using the library and the internet
- ability to write macros in Visual Basic for Applications (VBA) to add functionality to an existing Microsoft program, in order to meet some specific requirement that the macros and routines in these programmes do not already cover
- developing and maintaining schedules
- developing prospectus documents
- handling client telephone calls confidently and reliably
- developing and overseeing the production of pitch books.

Pitch books are presentation packs, usually prepared in PowerPoint and then printed out for client meetings. They have to be absolutely accurate, with no spelling, punctuation or mathematical errors; all figures must be accurate and their sources listed, all specifics and no generalities. They are created using some standard information and templates, but they have to be signed off by the assignment management hierarchy above you, usually an Associate, VP and MD. Naturally, they will usually make a lot of changes, which will often conflict with each other and which, due to the pressures of work, will often be given to the Associate to resolve, check for accuracy and incorporate at the last minute. This is just one example of why the hours can be very long.

The three main types are:

1. **Market overviews/bank introductions:** designed to give the client basic information on the bank itself and the subject matter you are there to discuss. In other words it is designed to prove to the client

that you know what you are talking about and have some credible track record.

2. **Deal pitches:** these are more critical. A client may shortlist several banks to present to them how they would undertake a specific project and how much they propose to charge. The aim of the pitch book is to make a compelling case that the client should choose your bank, forming the foundation against which the meeting will take place and against which the senior sales people from your bank will talk.

3. **Management presentations:** these are created for clients you already work for to promote their company to investors or potential buyers. They are less quantitative and more focused on the strengths of your client's business.

The key to understanding why this is hard work is that *everything* has to be right, *everything* has to be ready when needed and *everything* has to be of outstanding quality. This is complicated by the fact that a lot of the elements of your work are outside your direct control and will require negotiation with colleagues and (diplomatic) chasing of senior people to get the information you need to do your job properly. There are no compromises on any of these factors as they could result in massive financial consequences for the firm you work for.

According to Analysts, the keys to success include:

- getting the job done to time, to quality and to budget without complaint
- the flexibility and stamina to do very long hours as necessary
- taking on as much as you possibly can, without the risk of failures
- asking for help when you need it and being helpful to others when you can
- getting on well with colleagues and bosses
- networking effectively – but don't gossip
- having a positive mental attitude and an outgoing personality
- dressing neatly.

Associate

The general skill set for an Associate includes:

- ensuring the accuracy and quality of the work of any Analysts assigned to work with you on projects, in terms of financial models, PowerPoint presentations, multiples, correspondence etc.
- prioritising and allocating work: Associates will receive requests or instructions from a range of senior people in the firm – AVPs, VPs, Directors and Managing Directors – and a lot of their time will be spent liaising with various people and services, in person, on the phone and by email, to ensure that everything necessary gets done and done properly
- complex financial modelling, particularly in live cases where their work will be viewed by the VPs
- ability to build an effective and productive internal network with the relevant key people in middle and back office services, such as ICT specialists, lawyers, messengers, librarians and compliance managers.

The skill set for Associates in investment banking, corporate finance and M&A includes:

- outstanding skills with Excel
- ability to accurately assess the attractiveness of an investment opportunity using discounted cash flow (DCF) valuations
- ability to find and identify comparable companies
- ability to arrange high-level client meetings and have their logistics run smoothly
- a high level of influencing and persuasion skills, particularly the effective handling of very strong characters with definite views.

The skill set for Associates in debt and equity capital markets includes:

- ability to accurately track past deals and pricing to accurately predict where the market is going
- ability to rapidly and accurately price up new deals, such as convertibles, bonds and preferreds
- instilling confidence in clients
- generating and checking weekly newsletters
- making a constructive contribution to client meetings, although their input is usually restricted to talking about 'the numbers'

- co-ordinating due diligence investigations
- preparing documentation for debt and equity deals
- generating complex pitch books rapidly and accurately.

The skill set for Associates in sales and trading positions includes the ability to:

- know where relevant prices are at all times
- prepare option pricing models rapidly and accurately
- make clients feel confident in your abilities
- socialise constructively (e.g. during golf or tennis) with clients and build relationships with them.

According to Associates, the keys to success include:

- getting the job done to time, to quality and to budget, including your own and everyone else's work
- the flexibility and stamina to do very long hours as necessary
- identifying where a job or a process could be done better and developing a new way to achieve that
- being seen to use your initiative and make continual progress
- developing a reputation for reliability
- becoming the 'go to' person for solving superiors' problems.

Accountancy

Trainee Accountant

The key skills include:

- an excellent understanding of the principles of accountancy
- excellent skills with Excel spreadsheets, MS Word, PowerPoint
- handling client telephone calls confidently and reliably
- work prioritisation and planning – balancing conflicting deadlines and changing timetables
- a high level of financial numeracy and an ability to use statistics
- good communication skills, both written (concise, thorough reports) and oral (excellent in meetings and persuasive presentation skills)
- ability to build an effective and productive internal network with the relevant key people

- ability to communicate effectively and build long-term working relationships with existing and potential clients
- ability to negotiate, solve problems and make effective decisions
- high levels of integrity and honesty
- ability to work productively and harmoniously as part of a team
- ability to adapt to change
- good social skills to mix with the culture of your employer and your clients
- high levels of self-motivation to successfully study for and pass complex and difficult exams while working effectively in your substantive job
- ability to work on more than one project at once and complete them all successfully
- ability to work alone or as part of a team.

According to accountancy trainees, the keys to success include:

- getting the assigned tasks done to time, to quality and to budget without complaint
- taking on as much as you can possibly do, without the risk of failure – which means being able to (very occasionally) say no when asked to take something on
- asking for help when you need it and being helpful to others when you can
- getting on well with colleagues and bosses
- making sure you keep up with your studies, getting all homework completed in your own time
- fitting in well with the company culture.

Management consultancy

The key skills of a trainee Management Consultant include:

- excellent skills with Excel spreadsheets, MS Word, PowerPoint
- work prioritisation and planning – balancing conflicting deadlines and changing timetables
- ability to inspire confidence in clients
- a good level of financial numeracy and an ability to use statistics

- excellent communication skills, both written (concise, thorough reports) and oral (effective in meetings and highly persuasive presentation skills)
- ability to build an effective and productive internal network with the relevant key people
- ability to communicate effectively and build long-term working relationships with existing and potential clients
- ability to negotiate, solve problems and make effective decisions
- ability to understand how organisations and businesses work and how people in them behave
- an understanding of the industry sector in which you will be working
- ability to think in a structured/critical way to analyse problems, find solutions and communicate them persuasively to clients
- close attention to detail coupled with an eye for the big picture.

According to consultancy trainees, the keys to success include:

- getting the assigned tasks done to time, to quality and to budget without complaint
- the flexibility and stamina to do very long hours as necessary
- the flexibility to work at different client locations around the country for extended periods as necessary
- taking on as much as you possibly can, without the risk of failure – which means being able to (very occasionally) say no when asked to take something on
- asking for help when you need it and being helpful to others when you can
- getting on well with colleagues and bosses
- fitting in well with the company culture.

The offer

When the offer comes it can be overwhelming. It is tempting to just throw your hands in the air and celebrate the end of the long, difficult process, but you need to study your offer very carefully.

Formal job offers, whether conditional or unconditional (for example depending on exam success and grade), should be made in writing. Even if the main details are discussed in person first, or you are told in person of a decision to make an offer, a formal offer letter should follow. The offer letter should also include a full set of any terms or conditions of employment that apply to the job, as it will be the basis of a legal contract between you and your employer.

First you need to check the job title. Within organisations, a lot will be read into your job title and you need it to be appropriate and what you expected. If you are, for example, offered the money you want but your title is 'junior' something instead of the expected 'senior' something – is this still okay with you, bearing in mind that this title will live on forever in your CV?

You also need to be happy with the role being offered, the salary and package of benefits, the location and the duration, if it is not permanent. Would you be studying for a professional qualification? If so, which one? What happens if you fail any of the exams? Are you tied to the firm after qualification? If so, for how long? Does the firm have the right to decide where you work? If it decides to send you abroad for a long period, do you have the right to say no? If it is a permanent offer of employment, how long is the notice period? (You want that to be as long as possible.) Finally, how long do you have to make a decision?

Approach this as if it were another test. Work out what aspects are important and if any are deal-breakers. Work out how much you want that specific job. You need to be sure, because your acceptance of an offer is legally binding, so if you are not clear on any aspect of the offer, request clarification.

Often a position has a fixed salary and that is what everybody gets. On the other hand, it is sometimes possible to negotiate the terms of the offer. You may be asked directly, for example, how much you want in the way of salary. Do your research and think about that, particularly before any interviews, as you don't want to dither when asked. Have a reasonable figure in mind that you would be happy with and ask for it. You can phrase this non-confrontationally, for example by saying something like, 'My first thoughts are that I would be looking for a figure in the region of . . ., but that would depend on the situation relating to bonuses and benefits. How does that compare to what you had in mind?' That leaves the door open for haggling if needs be.

Another significant issue is whether or not you are expecting any other offers. If you get an offer shortly after starting a job hunt, for example if you start in autumn and get an offer around Christmas, most big graduate recruiters will understand that you may have other interviews lined up, so they may not be expecting an early acceptance. However, it is important to keep in touch with the firm that makes an offer and let them know what is happening, rather than keeping them in the dark. Write to the employer to acknowledge the job offer and indicate when you will get back to them with your decision. Keep your correspondence professional and be tactful (don't, for example, say you're hoping something better might come along!).

If you do get more than one offer, the ideal situation is to wait until you have them all and assess them against each other before deciding. In real life you may not have that luxury, but at least think carefully before signing on the dotted line, as this will shape your life for the next few years – one way or another.

8

Training and development: what to expect

Different employers will have different plans for training and developing new staff. In general, these plans will, in all sectors, be in line with the size and stature of the firm and the nature of the role.

The larger the firm, the more likely it is that there will be either a formal training and development programme or at least some form of sponsored support for working towards professional qualifications. Smaller firms are more likely to expect people to arrive who are ready to be immediately productive. This also means that it is less likely that any training will be provided beyond the minimum necessary for the specific role. Study for professional qualifications, for example, may be entirely in your own time.

The larger firms that run graduate entry schemes involving professional qualifications will also require trainees to commit to the firm for a period of years after qualification – to get the benefit of their investment.

The way in which in-house training is delivered is also likely to differ according to the size of the firm. The big companies will probably have formal programmes, away days and development groups working to standard formats, including assessment. They will also sometimes have an inbuilt waiting time of perhaps six months for these programmes, to avoid spending training time and effort on those who, for whatever reason, do not stay with the firm. Smaller firms as well as larger ones will often adopt a mentor system, assigning new employees an established member of staff with whom they can work on certain projects or tasks and to whom they can refer if they have questions.

Professional qualifications

These are the main professional qualifications required for each sector.

Retail banking

A lot depends on the career you select within retail banking, but the key qualifications (which are UK-specific) are examined by the ifs School of Finance, which is a not-for-profit professional body and registered charity incorporated by royal charter. The qualifications are as follows.

Personal Bankers/Customer Advisers/Bank Managers

- **Certificate in Regulated General Insurance (CeRGI).** For these non-regulated roles, the usual requirement is for staff to study for the CeRGI at the start of their career. CeRGI covers home insurance, car insurance, contents insurance, travel insurance and all the other products customers are offered when opening a new current account. This basic qualification enables a Personal Banker to offer a full and consultative service to their customers.
- **Banking and Finance Degree – BSc (Hons).** Many universities offer banking and finance related degrees, sometimes including economics.

Other available qualifications include:

- Certificate in Supervising in a Regulated Environment (CeSRE)
- Certificate in Regulated Customer Care (CeRCC)
- Certificate in Regulated Complaints Handling (CeRCH)

- Finance and Banking MBA offered via the Chartered Banking Institute – also confers 'Chartered Banker' status.

Mortgage Adviser

- Mortgages are classified as 'regulated sales', which means that advisers must hold a mandatory qualification. The benchmark for the industry is the **Certificate in Mortgage Advice and Practice (CeMAP)**, which provides a 'licence to practice' by meeting the educational standard of the FSA. This qualification is also a requirement for studying the Level 4 **Diploma in Mortgage Advice and Practice (DipMAP)**, but this only serves to prove advanced education in the subject and, while it may be required for jobs at some levels in some banks, it is not a mandatory qualification in the way that CeMAP is.
- **Banking and Finance (BSc).** There are currently 22 colleges offering a full-time three-year degree course in Banking and Finance, which covers finance, economics, management and accounting. In addition to their obvious application in banking, this degree is also seen as useful for careers in, for example, procurement, journalism and financial advice.

Other available qualifications include:

- Certificate in Regulated Equity Release (CeRER).

Financial Advisers

This is another area of regulated sales with a mandatory qualification. As of 2012, as required by the FSA's Retail Distribution Review (RDR), any individual who wishes to advise customers on retail investment products will be required to hold a recognised Level 4 qualification. This is the **Diploma for Financial Advisers (DipFA)**. The diploma can be completed in nine months and is examined by the ifs School of Finance. It comprises two mandatory units: Financial Services Regulation and Ethics, and Advanced Financial Advice.

Investment Managers

The **Investment Management Certificate (IMC)** is an FSA-approved threshold competency examination that aims to ensure knowledge of the regulations and practices of financial markets, the categories of securities and the principles of investment management. The IMC is examined by the CFA Society of the UK (formerly UKSIP), an international, non-profit organisation of investment practitioners and academics. Some banking establishments will take on candidates who are not qualified (or are part-qualified) and will encourage and assist them to complete their studies, although this is often dependent on market conditions. It is more likely when the market is buoyant; when the market is tougher, clients will expect qualifications and commensurate levels of experience from day one.

For more information about qualifications in retail banking, see http://institute. ifslearning.ac.uk/Qualifications.

Organisation profile

ifs *School of Finance*
Incorporated by Royal Charter

The *ifs School of Finance* is a not-for-profit professional body and educational charity, incorporated by Royal Charter.

We have been educating financial services professionals for over 130 years and have an unrivalled reputation within the banking and financial services industry for producing graduates of the highest calibre, with a detailed understanding of the industry and the practical skills to apply that knowledge in the workplace.

The MSc in Banking Practice and Management and Chartered Fellowship is a unique, specialist postgraduate qualification for those aspiring to senior roles in banking and financial services.

The MSc is designed to provide you with the advanced knowledge, skills and analytical tools that are required to lead effectively in complex financial services organisations. We aim to give you an advantage in both the recruitment market and in the work place by developing your abilities and understanding and by giving you an opportunity to immerse yourself in the industry while you study.

Like all of our professional higher education qualifications the content and learning experience of the MSc is directly informed by what employers tell us they look for from potential recruits. The MSc bridges the academic/vocational divide to provide you with essential practical skills and the conceptual and analytical abilities of academic study.

It is this unique and innovative approach that makes the *ifs* the provider of choice for organisations and individuals seeking to improve the knowledge, skills and credentials necessary for a management career within a broad spectrum of financial services organisations.

Key features of the programmes include:

- highly relevant content, focusing on the topics of greatest importance in the current banking environment
- designed and delivered in collaboration with the financial services industry to ensure you develop the knowledge and skills required for a successful management career
- direct entry to the prestigious *ifs School of Finance* Chartered Fellowship
- study either full-time at our campus in the City of London or part-time through a combination of online distance learning and face-to-face workshops
- the knowledge and insight necessary to operate to the highest professional standards and differentiate yourself from your peers in the highly competitive, fast-moving world of financial services.

Holders of the *ifs* MSc in Banking Practice and Management are eligible to apply for Chartered Fellowship of the *ifs* upon demonstration of three years' relevant professional experience in financial services. A recognised mark of senior status within the industry, the Chartered Fellowship is only available to those individuals who complete a master's qualification with the *ifs*; Chartered Fellows are, therefore, a select group of individuals representing the pinnacle of academic and professional achievement in the field of financial services.

Visit www.ifslearning.ac.uk/MSc or call 01227 829499 to find out more.

Case study

David Farley began studying the MSc in Banking Practice and Management in January 2011, having successfully completed the BSc (Hons) in Financial Services and Associateship with the *ifs School of Finance* two years earlier.

A key factor for David choosing the *ifs* for part-time postgraduate study was his prior 'positive experience'. He says: 'Having studied previously towards a BSc with the *ifs*, taking this forward into an MSc was a natural choice to continue my development. The *ifs* is a professionally run organisation with a very clear focus on its stakeholders. I am not aware of any other organisation that is so closely aligned to developing and delivering increased professionalism in banking.'

How would you rate the quality of teaching on the MSc programme?

I have never been disappointed with the quality of tuition and materials from the *ifs*. The programmes are intended for professionals and are delivered with this very clearly in mind.

How beneficial has the MSc been to your role and organisation?

The course content and learning has been extremely beneficial. Being in a risk-related role, the programme has been 100% relevant and I have frequently been able to transfer learning into my job.

Would you recommend the *ifs* and the MSc programme to potential students?

I would recommend the *ifs* without question. Anybody working for a financial institution and seeking to develop themselves professionally would benefit from an *ifs* programme.

Investment banking

Graduate entry (normally to an Analyst position) is usually restricted to people holding at least a 2.i degree, usually in finance, economics or a related subject, from a good university. A second language is often an advantage. Similarly, new Associates will have an MBA or similar advanced qualification. People intending to work with the bank in a quantitative analytical or similar role will need a PhD or advanced degree in computing, physics, maths, mathematical finance, engineering or similar.

FSA approval

Those intending to be investment bankers must pass the exams set by the Chartered Institute for Securities and Investment (CISI) (www.cisi.org.uk), in order for the FSA (www.fsa.gov.uk), the universal British finance regulatory body, to approve them as an investment banker. These exams are usually taken after a graduate has been employed by the investment bank for around two months, during which time, in the larger banks, they will have been subject to an intense internal training programme, often with exams every week.

There are two related exams. Graduates need to pass the Regulations exam to speak to clients, and the Derivatives exams to deal in securities and derivatives respectively. It is possible to take these two exams either together or separately – which will typically be the bank's decision rather than the graduate's. There are also Certificates in Investment Management and Corporate Finance for those going down that route.

These exams are very important, not only for professional development, but because it is not unknown for investment banks to fire anyone who fails them twice. This may sound harsh but, as one FSA exam trainer put it:

> *"Why should they keep someone on who fails exams when there's a hundred people out there who could instantly fill their shoes?"*
>
> *FSA Exam Trainer (timelessthinking.blogspot.co.uk)*

It was reported recently that 35% of applicants fail at least one of these exams once.

The exam is a computer-based, multiple-choice exercise, rather like the DVLA driving theory exam. Unlike the DVLA, however, the CISI refuses to issue any sample questions or formal teaching content. Most London investment banks will use 7city (www.7city.com), Kaplan (www.kaplan.co.uk) or BPP (www.bppfinancialservices.com) to provide the reading material and classroom courses to help students pass the exams. They do this by sending trainers into exams, where they memorise as many questions as they can, come out and transcribe them.

The questions are extremely technical and focused on what some investment bankers subsequently describe as minutiae that they will not use in their real working lives. This is an actual example question from a couple of years ago:

> *"Products available on the CBOE include equity index options on the S&P 100 and the S&P 500. Which of the following is true with respect to the exercise style of these options?*
>
> *a) S&P 100 index options — American and European style, S&P 500 options — European style only*
>
> *b) S&P 100 index options — American and European style, S&P 500 options — American style only*

c) *S&P 100 index options – American style only, S&P 500 options – European style only*

d) *S&P 100 index options – European style only, S&P 500 options – European style only"*

However, regardless of their reputation, passing these exams is absolutely necessary for a career in this field.

Interestingly, it is possible to take these exams as a private individual if you pay for them yourself and some graduates do this in the summer holiday before actually joining an investment bank in order to make the next few months easier. The gamble, however, is that if you fail these exams three times as a private candidate, you will not be allowed to reapply for the next six weeks, which might present difficulties with the bank's timetable for training.

Other professional qualifications

Several investment bank graduate programmes also offer the chance to study to become a Chartered Accountant with the ICAEW, the Institute of Chartered Accountants of Scotland (ICAS) or the Chartered Accounts of Ireland (CAI).

After this, there is considerable in-house training in techniques, bank processes and systems, financial modelling, statistical analysis, etc. Beyond that, the training is largely on the job. You will learn from more experienced staff and acquire a detailed personal knowledge of the characteristics and mechanics of whatever aspect of investment banking you are involved in.

The extent to which this is formalised varies. At the top end, for example, Goldman Sachs has its own internal 'university' offering a wide range of courses and programmes relevant to the different careers in investment banking. Requirements are different for each division of the firm, but there is a general expectation that staff will undergo 10 hours' training per annum as a minimum, with an ideal of 20 hours. This can be done through classroom sessions, online learning, directed reading, etc. Similar models will be found in most of the major firms. In terms of the continuing professional development (CPD) requirements of many professional bodies, this is very light – perhaps one or two days.

Organisation profile: London School of Business and Finance (LSBF)

LSBF has campuses across the world, a huge range of specialist programmes, students from over 150 countries and an award-winning online platform – all founded on delivering success in business, accounting and finance.

From our very first programme in 2003, we brought innovation by combining ACCA qualifications with an MBA. This matched business skills with accounting excellence, and we've never looked back.

The number of ways we shape the financial leaders of tomorrow has grown over the last decade, but our dedication to delivering success hasn't faltered.

Flexible ACCA, CIMA and CFA® courses
Full-time or part-time, in class or online, our highly experienced tutors are there when you need them. Study at our daytime, evening or weekend classes, or whenever you like through our online platform. You can even blend in-class and online learning!

Award-winning online platform, powered by InterActive
Access HD recorded lectures covering the syllabus, and have live lectures streamed straight to your screen. These are backed by extensive study materials, such as notes, revision packages and mock exams. Dedicated tutors and a global community of students and mentors are also there for you.

Finance-oriented postgraduate courses
Our Global MBA lets you specialise in areas such as financial management and investment banking. You can also take an MSc Finance and Investment with specialist pathway options including Accounting and Financial Management, as well as Investment Banking and Capital Markets.

Undergraduate finance programmes
Our BSc (Hons) Financial Management can be tailored to meet your finance career goals. Specialist study pathways include Finance and Accounting, as well as Banking and Finance. We also offer a dedicated BA (Hons) Accounting and Financial Studies.

Study at a Global Campus™
We have city centre campuses in London, Manchester, Birmingham, Singapore and Toronto. This gives you the opportunity to match a globally recognised qualification with vital international experience and perspectives.

Combine your ACCA or CIMA qualification with an MBA
Take your career further and increase your earning potential by adding the advanced business skills of a Global MBA: Financial Management to your ACCA or CIMA qualification.

It can take as few as two extra modules plus a dissertation, and you gain two globally recognised qualifications.

Diplomas that match skills with experience

In partnership with London Metropolitan University, we provide a range of full-time accounting and financial management diplomas. Available at foundation, undergraduate and postgraduate levels, you benefit from unique work-based elements offering vital practical experience.

The diplomas also prepare you for ACCA or CIMA exam success, while the work-based modules offer an ACCA or CIMA Practical Experience Requirement (PER) head start.

Visit www.lsbf.org.uk/wic or call +44 (0) 203 005 6243 to discover how we can deliver success for you.

Case study

ACCA – Muhammad Luqman

Muhammad is a current ACCA student who has prepared for the first seven papers at LSBF and passed all papers successfully.

'LSBF is one of the greatest institutes in providing quality ACCA education in London. The school's staff is highly skilled and the tutors are friendly, approachable and always happy to answer questions, whether in class or after class.

'LSBF's course materials are an excellent source of information and have been incredibly helpful in helping me pass my exams. The class notes, revision kits and LSBF's InterActive platform are always up to date and very useful through the whole process of preparation for the ACCA exams.'

What's your advice for new students?

'My personal experience with LSBF is very good. I started my ACCA in LSBF and have passed all of the first seven papers thanks to the help of LSBF's tutors, such as Hafeez Qazi, Francis Braganza, Debbie Crossman and Rob Sowerby. I would recommend joining LSBF to prepare for ACCA.'

CIMA – Hanna Chappell

Hanna Chappell, an Accountant at Financial Express, went straight into working after finishing school at 18. Hanna studied for her ACCA qualification at LSBF.

'CIMA complemented my work and was what I needed to do to take my career to the next level. LSBF kept appearing when I was searching for colleges and there were very good recommendations on the site. This, paired with the very competitive price, small classes and online availability of lectures, made me choose LSBF.

'I enjoyed the whole course, I found the lecturers provided interesting notes and ways to make us learn the materials. I was also very impressed with the availability of lecturers; within a day of emailing them I would have a response.'

What advice would you give to new students?

'Definitely to keep up with the homework as you go along and doing questions helps so much, more than reading through.'

MBA – Baada Sama Foray

Baada began his finance career at PKF. He obtained his MBA at LSBF and is also a member of the Chartered Institute for Securities and Investments.

'At LSBF I've been exposed to good lectures given by tutors with a strong experienced background with the necessary qualifications. These tutors not only knew the material well but also delivered the information in a way that all students would understand.

'I believe I came out of this MBA a better professional with more confidence. Studying the MBA at LSBF taught me how to defend myself when presenting my work. The core modules taught me about operations management and organisational behaviour, amongst other things, which gave me the necessary skills to take on a more senior role in a company.'

Organisation profile   Tolley® Exam Training

Tolley Exam Training is one of the leading national training providers for tax qualifications. Through a combination of highly experienced tutors, quality training material and our unique online services, Tolley Exam Training offers the best study experience available. We consistently achieve exceptional pass rates that significantly surpass the national average – making it the natural choice when enrolling with a training provider in order to pursue a career in Taxation.

Tolley Exam Training offers:

- some of the most experienced and well known tutors in the country
- a proven track record for securing outstanding pass rates
- access to Tolley's Online Academy with study manuals, audiovisual lectures and student and tutor forums, meaning you can study anytime, anywhere
- Tolley's Performance Tracker, enabling you to view your study plan online and download practice exams and answers, allowing you to track your performance
- a free one-year subscription to Taxation magazine.

Exceptional pass rates

We consistently achieve outstanding pass rates that significantly surpass the national average and we are confident that we will continue to do so.

ATT May 2012 Examination

	Tolley Exam Training*	National average
Paper 1	97.7%	71.9%
Paper 2	96.8%	72.3%
Paper 3	100%	92.2%
Paper 4	100%	87.3%
Paper 5	100%	81.5%
Paper 6	83.3%	86.8%

* Students who have studied with our Guaranteed Pass Scheme.

CTA May 2012 Examination

	Tolley Exam Training*	National average
Awareness	98%	86%
Advisory	87%	44%
Application	94%	58%

* Students who have studied with our Guaranteed Pass Scheme.

Regional Training Centres

Due to the successful launch of our five regional training centres, we now offer classroom training at seven locations nationwide:

- Belfast
- Birmingham
- Bristol
- Edinburgh
- London
- Manchester
- Newcastle.

Qualifications offered

We are unique in the training market, being the only organisation that provides training exclusively for the professional tax examinations.

We offer training for the following examinations:

- Taxation Technician (ATT) – set by the Association of Taxation Technicians and aimed at those working in tax compliance
- Chartered Tax Adviser (CTA) – set by the Chartered Institute of Taxation and aimed at those wishing to become Tax Advisers
- ICAS Tax Qualification – set by the Institute of Chartered Accountants of Scotland and aimed at any tax professional working in a compliance or advisory role
- Advanced Diploma in International Taxation (ADIT) – set by the Chartered Institute of Taxation and aimed at those who want to further their careers in international tax
- Associate of the Institute of Indirect Taxation (AIIT) – set by the Institute of Indirect Taxation and aimed at those wishing to become Tax Advisers in the field of indirect taxation
- VAT Compliance Diploma (VCD) – set by the Institute of Indirect Taxation and aimed at those wishing to gain an entry-level qualification in, or improve their knowledge of, VAT.

Innovative study system

Guaranteed Pass Scheme – our experience and previous pass rates show us that students who follow the Tolley Exam Training programme have a very high chance of passing the examinations. As a result we have introduced the Guaranteed Pass Scheme. All students enrolled with us on this programme will be given one free correspondence and revision course, in the unlikely event that they fail their examinations.

Tolley's Online Academy allows you to study anytime, anywhere. You will be able to access all of our course manuals and questions banks via the Online Academy. You can view the audiovisual lectures online and download the audio files of the lectures to a media player. Help is never far away through the use of the tutor and student forums. The forums allow students to access our tutors' words of advice and to help build a study network by making contact with other students in different parts of the country.

The Online Academy is not only making studying more accessible, it is also making it simpler by having everything you need in one place. You can even access the legislation online, by using the links in the online manuals.

Tolley's Performance Tracker allows you full access to view your study programme and track your progress by comparing it with peers.

For more information on Tolley Exam Training please visit www.tolley.co.uk/examtraining, email examtraining@lexisnexis.co.uk or call 020 3364 4500.

Case study

Simon Groom is Director of Tax Training and Professional Development at Tolley, the UK tax division of LexisNexis.

All of a sudden tax is front page news, tax is no longer a boring subject never to be discussed, everyone has an opinion. No one can have missed the controversy around Jimmy Carr and his tax affairs, or the comments about members of Take That and the scheme they are said to have been involved in to reduce their tax bill. The Prime Minister is commenting publicly, and almost every journalist seems to want to have their say. People are divided but no one can deny that tax and accountancy is high profile at the moment and that it looks set to stay that way for some time to come.

So what is it all about and why should you consider a career in tax?

The debate is all around tax avoidance. We should establish at this stage that tax avoidance is legal, and there are no suggestions that those whose tax affairs have been discussed in the press were acting illegally in any way. The question being raised is whether how they acted was immoral.

If you were asked if you would like to legitimately reduce the amount of tax you pay, most people would say 'yes', as long as it was legal. Reducing your tax bill is tax avoidance, and therefore if most people would do it, it must be okay. But for most people, the scope for reducing your tax bill is limited, and you wouldn't want to pay someone a lot of money to advise you how to do it, so most of us don't bother to take advice.

If you are very wealthy, the opportunities for reducing your tax bill are greater, the amounts involved are much bigger, and therefore you might be prepared to pay someone to look at ways of reducing your tax bill. Surely in principle that's just the same as those of us who don't have lots of money; it just happens that the sums involved are bigger?

But now look at it another way. If there are people paying less tax it means the government has less to spend on public services, or reducing the deficit, and therefore might decide to raise additional tax elsewhere, by, for example, raising duty on petrol and diesel, meaning the ordinary person in the street pays more.

It's at that point that some people take a different view, and point to the inherent unfairness of it. They would argue that if the wealthy pay less tax the rest of us pay more. Unfair, immoral? I'll leave that for you to decide.

Whatever your opinion, there is no question that the government wants to go down the morality route, to try to shame people not to indulge in what they call 'aggressive tax planning'. The problem is, where do you draw the line? One person's aggressive tax planning might seem perfectly reasonable to another.

There is also no doubt that as tax becomes more complicated and the debate continues, the demand for tax advisers will grow.

All of a sudden, tax is sexy!

To find out more about getting the qualifications necessary for a career in tax visit www.tolley.co.uk/examtraining, call 020 3364 4500 or email examtraining@lexisnexis.co.uk.

Accountancy

This section gives a summary of accounting qualifications, but more detail can be found in *Working in Accountancy* by Sherridan Hughes and Natalie Sermon, published by Trotman.

There are four main types of accountancy qualification:

1. ACA (Associated Chartered Accountant)

2. ACCA (Association of Chartered Certified Accountants)

3. CIMA (Chartered Institute of Management Accountants)

4. CIPFA (Chartered Institute of Public Finance and Accountancy).

ACA (Associated Chartered Accountant)

This is the best recognised accountancy qualification in the UK and is examined by the ICAEW, one of the largest professional accounting bodies in Europe. The focus is primarily on tax and audit, but it does cover a range of other subjects.

The ACA entry requirements are two A levels and three GCSEs, including good grades in Maths and English, but the majority of students are graduates.

You can only study for this qualification if you already have a training contract with an employer prior to starting the course. A training contract usually means that your employer will pay for your course and all related expenses, but that you will be legally bound to work for that employer for between three and five years. The contract may include other clauses obliging you to, for example, repay all training costs to the employer if you leave before the end of the contract, or pass all the exams first time. Students are normally employed by accountancy practices. However, regardless of the employing organisation, the qualification itself is always the same.

Training takes a minimum of three years and requires that you complete 450 days of technical work experience and pass both examination stages – with 11 exams in total.

The ACA qualification comprises two stages, the Professional Stage and Advanced Stage modules. The 'knowledge' modules of the Professional Stage provide an introduction to the core concepts that underpin accountancy, and the 'application' modules demonstrate how the student can build on knowledge in practice. The Advanced Stage consists of two technical papers and a Case Study. There is integrated ethics training throughout to support business decision-making and there are specific ethics-related learning outcomes built into a number of modules.

This is a breakdown of a sample syllabus.

1. **The Professional Stage.**
    - Each knowledge module assessment is one and a half hours long and will be examined using computers, which will enable trainees and employers to schedule them at convenient times and dates. The

modules are: Management Information; Accounting; Law; Assurance; Principles of Taxation; and Business and Finance.
- Application modules require trainees to demonstrate their knowledge in a practical context. These modules will be assessed by paper-based examinations, each of which will be two and a half hours long. The modules are: Financial Management; Financial Accounting; Financial Reporting; Audit and Assurance; Taxation; and Business Strategy.

2. **The Advanced Stage.**
   - The Business Reporting Module requires trainees to apply technical knowledge and professional judgement to business scenarios taking a compliance approach.
   - The Business Change Module focuses on strategy, requiring trainees to demonstrate their planning skills and ability to give advice in a business context.
   - Both of these technical integration modules require trainees to apply their financial reporting, taxation, audit and assurance and ethics knowledge in an integrated manner.

3. **The Case Study.**
   - This is a four-hour paper and can be taken once both the technical integration modules have been attempted and the trainee is in the final year of their training contract.

You can find more detailed information at www.icaew.com.

ACCA (Association of Chartered Certified Accountants)

To qualify, you will have to pass three levels of examinations and complete a minimum of three years' experience in accounting or an approved accounting-related area. Most people complete the course in three years, but this can be extended to 10 years, after which you would be disqualified for taking too long.

This is a breakdown of a sample syllabus.

1. **Part 1**
   - Preparing Financial Statements
   - Financial Information for Management
   - Managing People

2. **Part 2**
   - Information Systems
   - Corporate and Business Law
   - Business Taxation
   - Financial Management and Control
   - Financial Reporting
   - Audit and Internal Review
3. **Part 3** Any two of the following:
   - Audit and Assurance Services
   - Advanced Taxation
   - Performance Management
   - Business Information Management
4. Three Core Papers:
   - Strategic Business Planning and Development
   - Advanced Corporate Reporting
   - Strategic Financial Management.

You can find more detailed information at www.uk.accaglobal.com.

CIMA (Chartered Institute of Management Accountants)

The CIMA qualification is focused on strategic and financial management issues.

To qualify, you will need to pass three levels of examinations and complete three years of practical experience with an employer. There are certain exemptions, listed on the CIMA website, available for people who already hold some accountancy qualifications. CIMA is relevant for non-accountants, especially business managers. It has little content relating to tax or audit, so it is not be relevant for people intending to specialise in those areas.

This is a breakdown of a sample syllabus.

1. **Financial Accounting Fundamentals:**
   - Conceptual and Regulatory Framework
   - Accounting Systems
   - Control of Accounting Systems
   - Preparation of Accounts

2. **Management Accounting Fundamentals:**
   - Cost Determination
   - Standard Costing
   - Costing and Accounting Systems
   - Marginal Costing and Decision-making
   - Budgeting
3. **Economics for Business:**
   - The Economy and the Growth of Economic Welfare
   - The Market System and the Competitive Process
   - The Macroeconomic Framework
   - The Open Economy
4. **Business Law:**
   - The English Legal System
   - Establishing Contractual Obligations
   - Performing the Contract
   - Contractual Breakdown
   - The Law of Employment
   - Company Formation
   - Corporate Administration
   - Corporate Finance
   - Corporate Management
5. **Business Mathematics:**
   - Basic Mathematics
   - Summarising and Analysing Data
   - Probability
   - Financial Mathematics
   - Forecasting

You can find more detailed information at www.cimaglobal.com.

CIPFA (Chartered Institute of Public Finance and Accountancy)

This is the most widely accepted accountancy qualification in the public sector. It generally takes three years to complete and comprises three stages.

1. **The Professional Certificate:**
   - Financial Accounting module
   - Management Accounting module

- Financial Reporting module
- Audit And Assurance module

2. **The Professional Diploma:**
   - Public Finance and Taxation module
   - Public Sector Financial Reporting module
   - Governance, Public Policy and Ethics syllabus
   - Financial Management syllabus
   - Business Strategy syllabus
   - Business Management syllabus

3. **Strategic:**
   - Strategic Leadership module
   - Strategic Financial Management module

On completing each stage, students acquire a recognised qualification. Each module is assessed in a three-hour exam. The CIPFA website contains full details of the different syllabuses for each module and sample exam papers for study purposes.

You can find more detailed information at www.cipfa.org.uk.

Management Consultancy

> "The majority of training takes place on the job – through personal learning and through mentoring and teaching from other members of the team (who are all very approachable). This ad hoc training is complemented by informal training sessions between consultants, where someone will explain a particular skill or technique, and more formal weekly training events with Consultants at the same level."
>
> Senior Consultant (www.targetjobs.co.uk)

Given the number of skill sets a Consultant can be required to have, there is no one recognised training route. Rather, a considerable number of qualifications can be appropriate, depending on the specialism and the sector of the Consultant. Here are some of the more common examples:

- Certificate in Management Consulting Essentials (Institute of Consulting (IC))

- Diploma in Management Consultancy (IC)
- accountancy qualifications: ACA; ACCA; CIMA; CIPFA
- actuarial qualifications: Institute and Faculty of Actuaries
- business administration qualifications: MScin Management Consultancy
- advanced professional degrees, e.g. PhD, MBA or master's degrees in Engineering, Science, etc., are specifically targeted by firms like McKinsey and the Boston Consulting Group.

The Certified Management Consultant (CMC) qualification is awarded to consulting professionals by The IC (www.iconsulting.org.uk) in recognition of a Consultant's experience, competence, skills and integrity. The qualification involves on-the-job assessment. Applicants provide a portfolio of evidence, submit questionnaires filled in by clients and then undergo a verbal assessment with two external assessors. This tests core technical and sector knowledge, builds essential skills for consultancy work including client-facing proficiency, and further develops general 'soft' skills such as independent working and analytical thinking.

To apply to become a CMC, applicants need to have at least three years' industry experience and be an IC member. As an industry-recognised badge of competence it serves as a reassurance to clients of the quality of the Consultant.

Earlier in a Consultant's career, they can also study for certificates and diplomas in management consulting offered by the IC. These provide an introduction to the sector and help develop key competences.

Professional bodies and associations

These are the main professional bodies and associations for each sector.

Retail banking

British Bankers' Association (BBA): www.bba.org.uk

This organisation styles itself as the voice of banking and financial services in the UK. It is a trade association and the representative organisation of Britain's banks.

Chartered Banker Institute: www.charteredbanker.com

This is the oldest banking institute in the world and the only remaining banking institute in the UK. It offers qualifications through partnership with Bangor University.

Institute of Financial Services (*ifs*): www.ifslearning.ac.uk

The institute examines for the key qualifications in retail banking, including the Certificate in Regulated General Insurance (CeRGI).

Investment Banking

Chartered Institute for Securities and Investment (CISI): www.cisi.org

The largest and most widely respected professional body for those working in the securities and investment industry in the UK.

Insurance

Chartered Insurance Institute (CII): www.cii.co.uk

This is the world's largest professional organisation for people who work in insurance, risk and financial services. As well as offering support to members at all stages of their career, it also sets exams for those in the profession from award and certificate level to chartered status and fellowship.

Accounting

Institute of Chartered Accountants in England and Wales (ICAEW): www.icaew.com

The professional body that issues the ACA qualification, which entitles people to call themselves a Chartered Accountant. It covers England and Wales.

Institute of Chartered Accountants in Scotland (ICAS): www.icas.com

The professional body that issues the CA qualification, which entitles people to call themselves a Chartered Accountant. It covers Scotland.

Association of Chartered Certified Accountants (ACCA): www.uk.accaglobal.com

The professional body that issues the ACCA qualification, which entitles people to call themselves a Chartered Certified Accountant.

Note: research has been unable to find any substantive difference between these three accountancy qualifications. The system appears to be similar to the different exam boards for GCSEs – the end qualification is effectively the same. The ACA and the CA appear to have slightly higher profiles, but the ACCA seems to be more widely recognised internationally.

Chartered Institute of Management Accountants (CIMA): www.cimaglobal.com

The professional body that issues the CIMA qualification, which entitles people to call themselves a 'Chartered Management Accountant'. This qualification is more orientated towards interpreting financial information to make business decisions.

Chartered Institute of Public Finance and Accountancy (CIPFA): www.cipfa.org

This is the world's only professional accountancy body to specialise in public services. Members work throughout the public services, in national audit agencies, in major accountancy firms, and in other bodies where public money needs to be effectively and efficiently managed.

Management consultancy

Institute of Consulting (IC): www.iconsulting.org.uk

This is the professional body for the consultancy profession. It is an organisation within the Chartered Institute of Management, the only chartered professional body that is dedicated to management and leadership. This body awards the Certified Management Consultant (CMC) qualification.

Management Consultancies Association (MCA): www.mca.org.uk

This is the representative body for larger management consultancy firms in the UK. The 45 member companies comprise around 60% of the UK consulting industry, employing around 30,000 consultants.

9

Other careers in the City

Of course, there are other careers for graduates in the City besides financial services, and there are many careers in financial services that do not rely on financial ability, skills or qualifications.

Financial institutions, like any large organisations, need a full range of support services to function effectively. These are sometimes seen as less glamorous than the customer-facing work of the organisations, but they are vital services without which these firms could not function effectively. Prime examples are HR, IT and sales and marketing.

There is even a specialist website that details vacancies across the financial service organisations – www.efinancialcareers.co.uk – which includes more than 30 different categories of jobs, including the examples listed above, each of which contains dozens of vacancies with different organisations.

HR

Investment banks, retail banks, hedge funds, private equity companies and management consultancies funds all need HR professionals to help manage their people – or their 'human capital'. Fundamentally, it is the role of the HR function in an organisation to help the organisation get optimum benefits from its investment in employing people. HR departments, for example, establish the framework within which people are employed, by developing policies, processes and pay scales.

Work in HR is both people- and process-driven. In the HR function in banks, on the one hand you are dealing with all the issues surrounding people in the workplace, and on the other you must help the bank comply with the legislation and regulations governing recruitment, employment and severance. For example, HR staff are responsible for ensuring there is no discrimination on the basis of race, age, gender or sexual orientation in a firm's recruitment, promotion or any other processes. They do this by establishing policies, designing processes and training managers in the operation of these arrangements in the workplace.

HR teams also have responsibility for administering annual performance appraisals. These are particularly significant in financial services, where the results of appraisals are an important factor in determining the size of employees' annual bonuses.

Although HR staff can be generalists (often called 'HR business partners'), many HR jobs are specialised. These include, for example, employee relations; industrial relations; graduate and general recruitment; compensation and benefits; and training and development.

The HR function is taken seriously by financial services organisations and several of those detailed in this book run graduate entry programmes specifically to find, train and retain top HR talent. This normally includes support for studying for professional qualifications.

IT

The right technology is often the factor that gives a financial services company the edge over its competitors. It can also, in the long run, help the organisation save money. Not surprisingly, therefore, firms in the financial sector are among the biggest investors in IT recruitment.

In an investment bank, for example, the really big user of technology is the trading floor and everything related to it. Whether it is a question of actually buying and selling financial products electronically, processing them through smart-order routing systems, or communicating to ensure that trades go through smoothly in the shortest time possible, vastly expensive technology projects are crucial to successful operations.

In financial services, IT careers tend to fall into one of these categories:

- development
- business analysis
- project management
- infrastructure
- technical support.

Developers are at the coalface of the IT department. One part of the job involves developing new systems in house, which offers opportunities for graduates with Java or other coding language skills. However, banks often purchase software off the shelf from third-party vendors. A developer's job will therefore also include tailoring that software to suit the institution's particular needs, or integrating it into their existing systems. There is often considerable pressure to achieve 'low latency', which means reducing the amount of time it takes to both execute and process transactions.

Business analysts act as the liaison between the IT department and the business side of the organisation, which often do not understand the complexities or terminology of each other's work. Business analysts have to understand exactly what is required by the internal end users and then investigate how technology can be used to improve the bank's competitive advantage.

Project managers will take charge of new projects once they are given the go-ahead. Project management roles are strategic and involve planning, structuring and completing projects to the satisfaction of their internal clients. Project managers work with a team of developers, liaise with third-party vendors as necessary and are answerable to the business should plans go awry.

Infrastructure roles deal with the nuts and bolts of IT – everything from servers to operating systems to databases.

Technical support roles involve solving problems when they arise with systems already in use, in other words things that should be working properly but aren't. This can be a minor bug fix or it can be a major problem that attracts media attention, such as the problems of Santander and Barclays Bank in the summer of 2012, which affected thousands of customers.

In addition to the graduate entry programmes run by the major firms, and the website given at the beginning of this chapter, there is also www.bankingjobsuk. co.uk, which holds details of hundreds of IT vacancies in financial institutions. It is worth noting that the graduate entry schemes will normally require a 2.i degree or better qualification in computer science or a related discipline, and potentially high-level coding skills.

Sales and marketing

These are the people who decide what the financial institutions should be trying to sell to their customers and who then try to persuade their customers to buy it. This also involves preparing marketing materials and business pitches to position the firm as it would like to be seen. From the level of their investment, it is clear that this is a vital function. For example, in recent years the top 10 retail banks in the UK have regularly spent around 5% of their revenue income on marketing. This function often also covers research into customer experiences to determine, for example, whether or not customers mind being served by contact centres and whether the location of those contact centres (i.e. whether they are in the UK or not) makes a difference.

In investment banks, salespeople advise clients, such as high net worth individuals, pension funds and hedge funds, on investment opportunities. These can be when to buy and when to sell securities. Financial salespeople usually focus on particular products such as government bonds, equities or derivatives. Larger investment firms employ research sales professionals who sell their employer's research expertise. There are also hybrid sales-traders, who recommend products to clients and then execute the trades resulting from their recommendations.

The marketing function of any organisation concerns itself with managing a firm's reputation by deciding how its brand name, products and services are portrayed in advertising and promotional campaigns. In banks, both retail and investment, marketing people not only promote their firms as a whole, but product-specific marketing people work alongside sales teams. A financial marketing career can include sponsoring events, producing brochures and other materials, developing corporate logos, determining the pricing and positioning of products and services, and researching markets for potential new products.

To succeed in a financial marketing job you should have strong written and oral communication skills, networking and relationship management capabilities, an understanding of and ability to communicate complex financial issues with authority and understanding, and have specific knowledge of markets and market segments.

Some of the larger firms employ graduates and have their own sales and marketing divisions. Others contract the work out to specialist organisations and agencies. In addition to the website listed at the beginning of this chapter, sites such as www.ambition.co.uk and www.simplyhired.co.uk also have specialist categories for sales and marketing vacancies in financial services organisations of various sizes.

10

Moving on

General considerations

Many people stay in the firm they start with for their entire career. Many don't – it all depends on the individual.

A lot of graduates will move between divisions within a large firm, or move to a different bank or firm. They might move to a larger firm in search of more money or promotion opportunities, or to a smaller one in search of greater personal recognition and a better work–life balance. This is something that often comes into sharp focus when children come along. A significant number of people eventually try to address this issue. As a big firm fee earner put it:

> *"You decide that the concept of 'enough' can actually be more important than the concept of 'more' and then you don't have to become a weekend parent . . ."*

This can be done by transferring to a smaller firm, where the hours might still be long in comparison to a baseline of nine to five, but are a lot shorter than big firm employees are used to.

Whatever the reasons for moving on, a big firm brand on your CV certainly does make you more credible in the job market.

Some people take their 'career planning' very seriously and work out how their life is meant to be for many years ahead. On the other hand, there are also those who would say planning your exit before even starting a career is of limited value, as you can never realistically predict what will happen and what opportunities will be available a few years down the line.

Retail banking

In the UK, the main retail banks are vast enterprises with the potential to provide many career paths. While a lot of the managerial and interpersonal skills of, for example, a Bank Manager are transferable to many companies, unless they are a qualified accountant their financial skills will only take them so far outside banking. For example, GPs' practices are often keen to hire people with bank managerial experience as Practice Managers and some of the larger practices can pay quite well. Alternatively, over 80% of the Chief Executives of charities come from the public and private sectors and banking would be a good background for that move.

There is also now the option to work for a community development finance institution (CDFI), which are independent financial organisations with a commitment to helping disadvantaged communities. They offer loans to social enterprises, small businesses, individuals and others who have been unable to secure funds from traditional banks, usually because of high risk or poor credit history. There are some 70 CDFIs across the country and they are seen as key players in the government's regeneration policy.

There are opportunities to move into financial positions with small to medium-sized enterprises or into the financial regulatory bodies.

Of course, as with all fields, there is always the choice of doing something radically different. As an example, a Bank Manager who moved from City work to become a Maths Teacher says:

"Making the move from the boardroom to the classroom has been one of the best things I've ever done. It's a real challenge, but bringing a subject like maths to life is much easier when you've got a practical background in it."

Bank Manager turned Maths Teacher

(www.careers.guardian.co.uk)

Investment banking

Analysts

Analysts typically stay at an investment bank for two or three years, but they often continue their career in financial services.

The best Analysts have the option of applying to the private equity firms, particularly if they have good experience of playing a significant role in live transactions. This can, however, still mean long hours if you join one of the bigger ones. Private equity firms also want Analysts with excellent financial modelling, valuation and other technical skills. In addition, it's important to demonstrate a solid understanding of the business side of things – in other words, knowing what are the key drivers of a company's growth, where are the risks, what types of cost might be excessive, etc. Last, but just as important, they want to hire Analysts with a high level of maturity and excellent communication skills. Analysts who move to private equity firms are generally given the job title of Associate.

Many Analysts join hedge funds. Their work in this field is more difficult to describe as hedge funds themselves can vary so wildly. They tend, however, to work market hours with limited weekend work, unless it is a hedge fund that acquires companies. There can also still be an element of travelling. Another alternative is to move into venture capital, or into a large company in another industry in a similar corporate development role. These options can offer a better lifestyle, albeit at a lower rate of pay than investment banking. Many Analysts leave to study for an MBA at a business school, either to change career entirely or to boost their prospects.

Associates

Associates are considered to have the potential for a long-term banking career, but a considerable number of them will still leave over time. Again, they often join hedge funds, but many join firms that they have been advising as a Banker. Some Associates either join start-ups or start their own business. However, as time goes by it becomes increasingly difficult for an Associate to make this transition, as they are specialising in specific investment banking skills that are less transferable. The one area where Associate opportunities are far more limited than those for Analysts is in private equity. These firms rarely hire Associates who were not previously Analysts or have not had private equity experience.

Working for a company in another field is a more common exit destination at the Associate level, because Associates are in search of a better lifestyle, because they do not wish to go further up the investment banking ladder, or simply because they want to work for a company that is actually 'making things' as opposed to simply providing advice.

Accountancy

Business has a continual need for good accountants and that isn't likely to change any time soon. A large proportion of the top financial management jobs in commerce and industry are filled by ex-big firm Accountants.

The first step can be to move from, say, external audit to internal audit at a client company, but other roles can include Financial Controller, Analyst or Manager. That said, in the first instance your new employer is probably going to want you to do something similar to what you have been doing the past few years, but you will also have the opportunity to evolve beyond that. As to what type of company might welcome you, that is in part determined by what sector you have been working in and the type and scale of the firm you are leaving. If you have been with a large accounting firm, you may find your skills are too specialised for smaller companies, and if you don't have experience of national-level companies as clients, a national-level company isn't likely to see you as a strong contender for direct employment. However, that still leaves a wealth of opportunities and different paths.

Management consultancy

Management consulting is an interesting career, so many who start in this role choose to remain in it for the duration of their working life, sometimes moving from larger firms to smaller consultancies or vice versa. Frequently, Consultants go freelance and offer their business consultancy services independently. Another common transition is into the higher management of clients companies or public sector bodies.

The skills learned in consulting are valuable to the general business community. Being able to build successful client relationships, having excellent persuasion skills, thinking in a structured manner, having highly honed and multidimensional problem-solving skills, coupled with a wide practical experience of different industries and client organisations, makes for a valuable package.

However, this normally needs to be done within the first three to five years of consulting. After this point employers may start to assume that such a varied environment will mean that someone will not be able to 'settle' into a permanent position with a more stable routine.

On the other hand, it is not unknown for people to join or re-join consulting after some years in an industry, but the same three- to five-year threshold still tends to apply.

Some final thoughts

Becoming 'something in the City' will require dedication, hard work and personal resolve, but working there can be exciting, fulfilling and extremely lucrative.

It can be a great career in its own right or an impressive springboard into many other spheres of business.

Hopefully, the facts, figures, advice and reference materials in this book will help you make your decision about your future career and assist you in getting there.

Glossary of terms

ACA Associate of the Institute of Chartered Accountants

ACCA Association of Chartered Certified Accountants

Actuary (actuarial) Actuaries mathematically evaluate the likelihood of events and quantify the probable outcomes in order to minimise losses for a financial organisation if uncertain 'undesirable' events take place

Analyst Common job title for a new graduate joining a financial institution. Originally applied to investment banks, but has recently become a popular term in retail banking, accountancy and management consultancy

Analytics Generic term for all the different techniques of analysis

Assessment centre A one-day or half-day event comprising a range of simulations of work at an employer, together with psychometric tests and interviews to enable employers to assess the strengths and weaknesses of applicants' performance in a group situation

Associate Common job title for the lowest level of 'professional' or direct fee-earning staff in a financial institution. Originally applied to investment banks, but has recently become a popular term in retail banking, accountancy and management consultancy

Audit Examination and verification of a company's financial and accounting records and supporting documents

AVP Assistant Vice President – a job title (usually in an American firm) indicating a middle manager

Back office General term for all departments of a business that do not deal with clients, but provide the

	infrastructure and services that the firm needs in order to operate (e.g. IT, HR, regulatory compliance)
Bloomberg	A provider of 24-hour global financial news and information including real-time and historic price data and trading news
Bond	A financial instrument (a legal agreement) in which the borrower promises to repay the money borrowed, plus interest, at some specific date in the future
'Buddy' or 'buddy system'	The practice of assigning an existing member of staff to be a personal point of contact for a new starter or intern, to make themselves available for questions about the firm and generally ease the new person into working effectively
Bulge bracket	The largest and most successful investment banks
Buy side	The department of an investment bank that works with clients wishing to invest, by advising them how to maximise their return when trading or investing in stocks, bonds or other securities
C++ and C#	Computer programming languages
CEO	Chief Executive Officer
CeRGI	Certificate in Regulated General Insurance
CFA	Chartered Financial Analyst
Channels	In the context of a financial institution, this refers to the different ways in which customers can communicate with and buy from the institution
CIMA	Chartered Institute of Management Accountants
CIPFS	Chartered Institute of Public Finance and Accountancy
Commercial banks	Banks dealing with medium to large commercial companies
Commodities market	A market where raw or primary products (e.g. oil, silver) are exchanged

Credit risk	The risk of loss of money through a person or organisation not being able to repay a loan made to them
Debt capital	The capital that a business raises by taking out a loan
Due diligence	The process of making all prudent and reasonable enquiries on behalf of your client to be satisfied that the proposed purchase of another company or any proposed merger is actually a sensible business deal in their best interests
Equity capital	Capital, in the form of stock or surplus earnings, that is free of debt, for example capital received for an interest in the ownership of a business
E-tray exercise (similar to a virtual office exercise)	An assessment tool for job applicants. It involves dealing with a set of simulated incoming emails as if you were on a real job. This is basically an update of a very old selection exercise called the 'in-tray exercise'
FD	Financial Director
Financial instrument	Packages of capital, each with its own unique characteristics and structure and often created by banks, which can be bought and sold
Financial modelling	Building spreadsheets that try to reflect the likely real-world financial impact of different circumstances, allowing the user to try out different scenarios to enable them to know what to do to get the result they want
Forensic accounting	An accountancy investigation of financial procedures that have been challenged or are alleged to be illegal
Front office	Departments of an investment bank working directly with clients and generating income for the bank
FSA	Financial Services Authority
FX	Short for Forex, which is short for foreign exchange
General studies	An A level qualification not generally accepted as counting towards the academic entry qualifications for internships or employment by the firms dealt with in this book

Glass-Steagall Act	US legislation that forcibly divided the business of deposit taking and loans from capital market businesses, or 'investment banking'
Hedge fund	An investment fund that can make a wider range of investments and trades than other funds, but which is only forparticular types of investor and is specified by regulators
High net worth clients	Very wealthy customers
Hot desking	Management policy of having fewer work stations than fee-earning, mobile staff – so people may work at a different desk with different neighbours each day they are in the office
HR	Human resources, the function of a firm dealing with matters relating to their employees. Also known as 'talent management', 'human capital' and 'personnel'
ICAS	Institute of Chartered Accountants in Scotland
Internship	A period of employment with a firm, normally a summer job or a sandwich work experience year, while the employee is still in full-time education – usually studying for a degree. This period of employment is often a formal programme designed to show what working at the firm is actually like and to give the person an understanding of the firm and its business
Investment bank	A bank that helps clients access the capital markets (such as the stock market or the bond market) to raise money for expansion, mergers and acquisitions, or for other purposes
Liquidity	In accounting, the ability of a person or organisation to pay their debts when they are due (e.g. bills or loans)
Matlab	A computer programming language
MBA	Master's degree in Business Administration – a popular postgraduate degree, seen as a general grounding for a business career. The quality of the MBA is judged by the reputation of the school awarding the qualification

M&A	Mergers and acquisitions, a function of investment banking in which the bank helps a client find a suitable 'target' firm to buy or merge with
MD	Managing Director
Mentor	A person acting as a personal career adviser to a younger or less experienced person in the same type of business
Middle office	Departments of an investment bank that control and monitor the bank's use of funds, levels of reserves, flows on money in and out, etc.
MIT	Massachusetts Institute of Technology
MORSE	A degree qualification in Mathematics, Operational Research, Statistics and Economics
Mutual fund	An open-ended fund run by an investment company that raises money from shareholders and invests it, in accordance with a stated set of objectives
Non-exec	Non-executive Director – a person on the board of a company or organisation who offers advice and guidance, but has no direct reporting staff and is not responsible for any specific aspect of the enterprise
Numerical reasoning test	A test of applicants' skill with numbers
Off-cycle internships	Internships that are set up on an 'as and when' basis, determined by when a good applicant makes contact, not according to a set timetable
Outsourcing	The practice of externalising what used to be an internal function within an organisation, e.g. employing another company to provide back office functions such as HR, IT, etc.
Private banks	Banks exclusively for a limited number of very wealthy clients, often off-shore
Proprietary trading	Where a bank trader invests or trades the investment(relates to 'prop trading' bank's own money for the bank's own private account and 'prop house')

Psychometric tests   Tests for employment applicants which purport to be able to predict the personality of the applicant and thus their performance in a given job.

Public practice firm   Accountancy firm offering services to clients

Quantitative analysis   Advanced and complex financial modelling, particularly used for the measurement, performance evaluation or valuation of a financial instrument

Retail bank   A banking institution that deals directly with individuals and small businesses, rather than with corporations or other banks

Rotational programme   A programme such as an internship, where the person 'rotates' through several placements in different parts of the organisation to better understand the business

Sandwich course   University courses that offer alternating periods of study and work experience (for up to a year)

Sell-on   Additional work sold to a client during a pre-existing project

Sell side   The departments in an investment bank that create and sell financial instruments, e.g. bonds, on behalf of clients

Situational judgement test   A test for job applicants that presents hypothetical challenging situations that they may encounter at work as an employee to evaluate how they respond

Strats   Strategists

UCAS points   The Universities and Colleges Admissions Service's tariff system that allows qualifications to be converted into points (e.g. an A at A level is worth 120 points) and then added together to give totals that can be used as a requirement to get into a course or as application criteria for a job

Universal banks   Banks covering retail, commercial and investment banking

Verbal reasoning test   A test of a job applicant's language ability

Virtual office exercise
(similar to an e-tray
exercise)

An assessment tool for job applicants. It involves dealing with a set of simulated incoming emails, notes and voicemails as if this were a day on a real job. An update of a very old selection exercise called the 'in-tray exercise'

VP

Vice President – a job title (usually in an American firm) indicating a middle manager or junior Director

Work experience

A period of time working for a company with the intention of understanding the firm and the business it is in, often in a structured programme. The term can apply to a few days or as much as a year with a company

Appendix 1

Significant boutique investment banks in London

These are the boutique investment banks located in London that have an M&A department. They usually work on smaller deals, normally below a billion dollars in value.

Firm	Comment	Contact details
RFC Ambrian (previously Ambrian Capital) 'We consider tertiary qualifications as a minimum but look for people from all backgrounds'	Mining, oil & gas, cleantech and life sciences sector – corporate finance and stockbroking	Old Change House 128 Queen Victoria Street London EC4V 4BJ Tel: 020 7634 4700 careers@rfcambrian.com
Arma Partners Graduate recruitment 'Junior bankers are expected to take on responsibility and to be involved in all aspects of the M&A and financial advisory process'	Technology, media and telecoms (TMT) sector – corporate finance advisory services	16 Berkeley Street London W1J 8DZ Tel: 020 7290 8100 recruitment@armapartners.com
Blackstone Group International Partners plc 'We are guided by a set of principles: Accountability, Excellence, Integrity, Teamwork and Entrepreneurship'	Large firm: London office specialises in private equity, real estate, advisory and restructuring services	40 Berkeley Square London, W1J 5AL Tel: 020 7451 4000 info@blackstone.com

Firm	Comment	Contact details
Brewin Dolphin 'We employ around 1,900 staff in our network of 41 offices across the UK and Channel Islands'	Provides independent financial advice and investment management services for private clients, pension funds, trusts and charities	12 Smithfield Street London EC1A 9BD Tel: 020 7246 1000 personnel@brewin.co.uk
Brown Brothers Harriman Investor Services Ltd 'We have a deep respect for a healthy work–life balance'	Oldest and largest private bank in the USA; 4,000 thousand staff globally, with an increasing focus on investment banking	Park House 16–18 Finsbury Circus London EC2M 7EB Tel: 020 7588 6166 Email contact via forms on website: www.bbh.com
CanaccordGenuity Ltd (formerly Hawkpoint) 'We operate in 24 cities worldwide and list companies on 10 stock exchanges'	Global investment bank focused on growth companies; Hawkpoint has a very good reputation	88 Wood Street London EC2V 7QR Tel: 020 7523 8000 recruitment@canaccordgenuity-hawkpoint.com
Evercore Partners 'We recruit top performers, exceptional academic record coupled with achieved work–life balance'	Investment banking advisory services – $1 trillion in announced transactions. Investment management services – $13 billion in assets managed	15 Stanhope Gate London W1K 1LN Tel: 02076536000 Graduate application using forms on the website: www.evercore.com
Espírito Santo Investment Bank (formerly Execution Noble) 'We are proud of the strong family values that govern the way we look after our clients, our colleagues and our community'	Investment bank and securities firm focused on large- and mid-cap pan-European, Brazilian and Polish secondary equities and research	BancoEspírito Santo de Investimento, SA London Stock Exchange Building 10 Paternoster Square, 3rd floor London EC4M 7AL Tel: 020 7456 9191 graduates@execution-noble.com
GleacherShacklock LLP 'As an Analyst at GleacherShacklock, early responsibility and greater exposure mean we require candidates who will thrive in a fast-paced entrepreneurial with outstanding analytical capabilities and commercial awareness'	Small UK boutique of 45 staff specialising in client-focused discreet advice on corporate finance matters. They do not provide financing products, distribute securities or publish research	Cleveland House 33 King Street London SW1Y 6RJ Tel: 020 7484 1150; 020 3008 2594 (recruitment) gleachershacklock@smithhoward.co.uk
Greenhill & Co 'We are interested in candidates with strong academic backgrounds and analytical abilities with communication skills, leadership ability and teamwork orientation'	Investment bank providing financial advice on M&A, restructurings, financings and capital raising to corporations, partnerships, institutions and governments	Lansdowne House 57 Berkeley Square London W1J 6ER Tel: 020 7198 7400 Greenhill@freshminds.co.uk (recruitment)
GCA Savian	Independent investment banking to technology, media, communications, healthcare, consumer and retail, and industrial sectors	Eagle House 108–110 Jermyn Street London SW1Y 6RH Tel: 020 70383200

Firm	Comment	Contact details
Harris Williams &Co 'Our firm's strong, consistent growth and senior leadership provide stability, a terrific culture, and significant career opportunities'	American middle market investment bank – M&A	63 Brook Street London W1K 4HS Tel: 020 7518 8900 careers@harriswilliams.com
HoulihanLokey 'We provide thoughtful, caring advice while acting with honour and integrity'	American investment bank with a strong reputation in restructuring	83 Pall Mall London SW1Y 5ES Tel: 020 7839 3355 Applications through the careers page of their website, www.hlhz.com
Liberium Capital 'We are truly independent with the business being owned 100% by staff'	London and NY-based boutique investment bank with about 130 staff	Ropemaker Place, Level 12 25 Ropemaker Street London EC2Y 9LY Tel: +44(0)20 3100 2000 Careers@liberumcapital.com
Panmure Gordon & Co.	Offices in London and San Francisco; known for technology transactions	155 Moorgate London EC2M 6XB Tel: 020 7459 3600
Perella Weinberg Partners 'Every person in the Firm should be devoted, first and foremost, to the Firm's reputation and well-being'	Prestigious boutique, founded by M&A specialists Joseph Perella and Peter Weinberg (ex-CEO of Goldman Sachs)	20 Grafton Street London W1S 4DZ Tel: 020 7268 2800 Application details on the careers page of the website, www.pwpartners.com
Piper Jaffray Ltd 'Great people working together as a team are our competitive advantage'	Large American boutique bank with offices in London	13th Floor 88 Wood Street London EC2V 7RS Tel: 0207 796 8400
Seymour Pierce 'Our culture is decidedly entrepreneurial, yet equally balanced by pragmatism and a sense of etiquette'	London-based boutique investment bank with a good reputation in equity research and an M&A team	20 Old Bailey London EC4M 7EN Tel: 020 7107 8000 enquiries@seymourpierce.com
William Blair International Ltd 'Our firm is consistently rated as one of the best places to work in the investment industry'	Headquarters in Chicago, with strong London presence	The Broadgate Tower 20 Primrose Street, 17th Floor London EC2A 2EW Tel: 020 7868 4440 recruitingdirector@williamblair.com Applications online, using their portal; website www.williamblair.com
McQueen Limited 'High quality, bespoke advice from senior and experienced practitioners'	Small London boutique investment bank (24 professional staff) focused on consumer, retail and leisure sectors	50 Pall Mall London SW1Y 5JH Tel: 020 7484 8800 contact@mcqueenltd.com

Index of advertisers